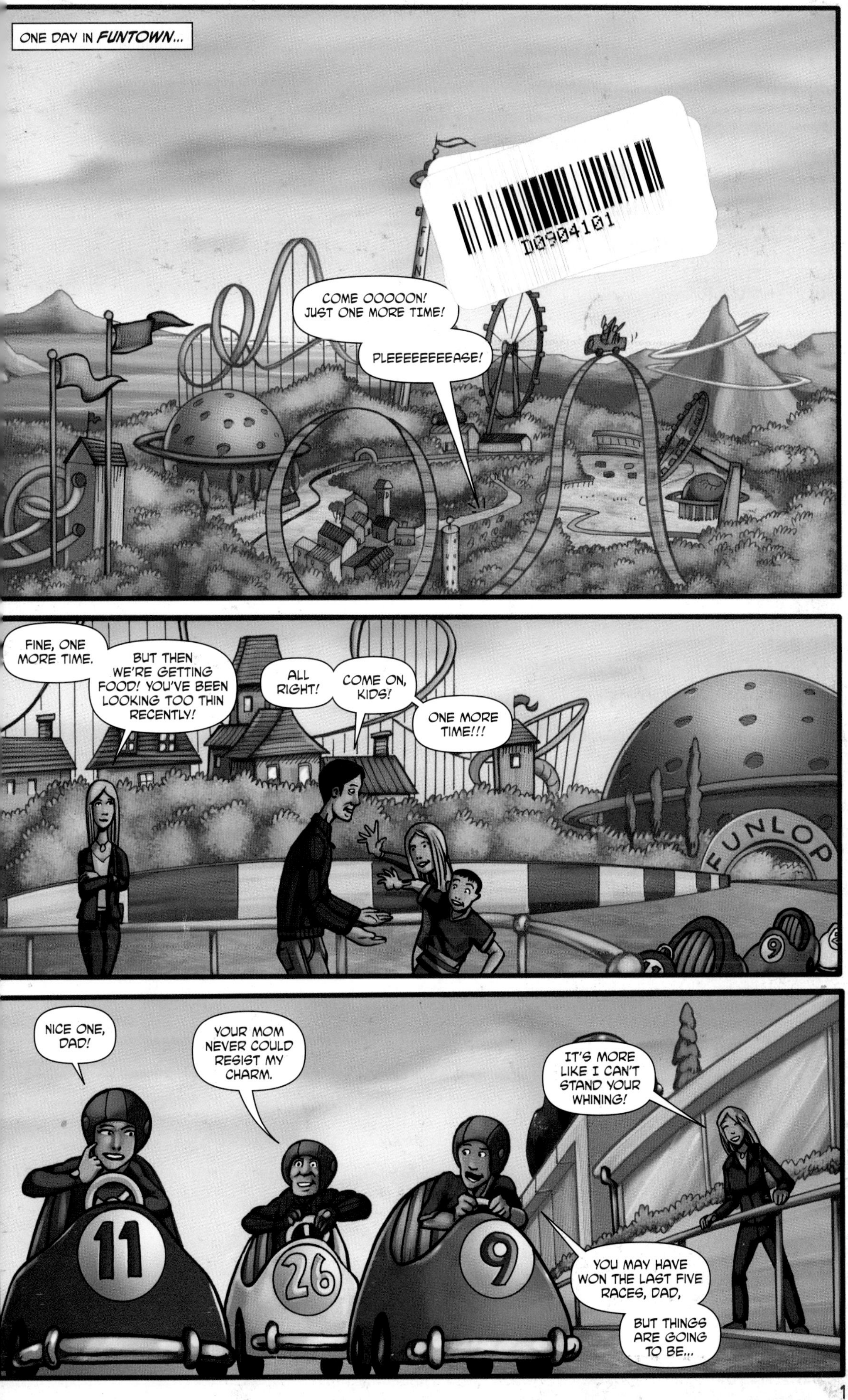
ONE DAY IN *FUNTOWN*...
COME OOOOON! JUST ONE MORE TIME!
PLEEEEEEEEASE!
FINE, ONE MORE TIME.
BUT THEN WE'RE GETTING FOOD! YOU'VE BEEN LOOKING TOO THIN RECENTLY!
ALL RIGHT!
COME ON, KIDS!
ONE MORE TIME!!!
FUNLOP
NICE ONE, DAD!
YOUR MOM NEVER COULD RESIST MY CHARM.
IT'S MORE LIKE I CAN'T STAND YOUR WHINING!
YOU MAY HAVE WON THE LAST FIVE RACES, DAD,
BUT THINGS ARE GOING TO BE...

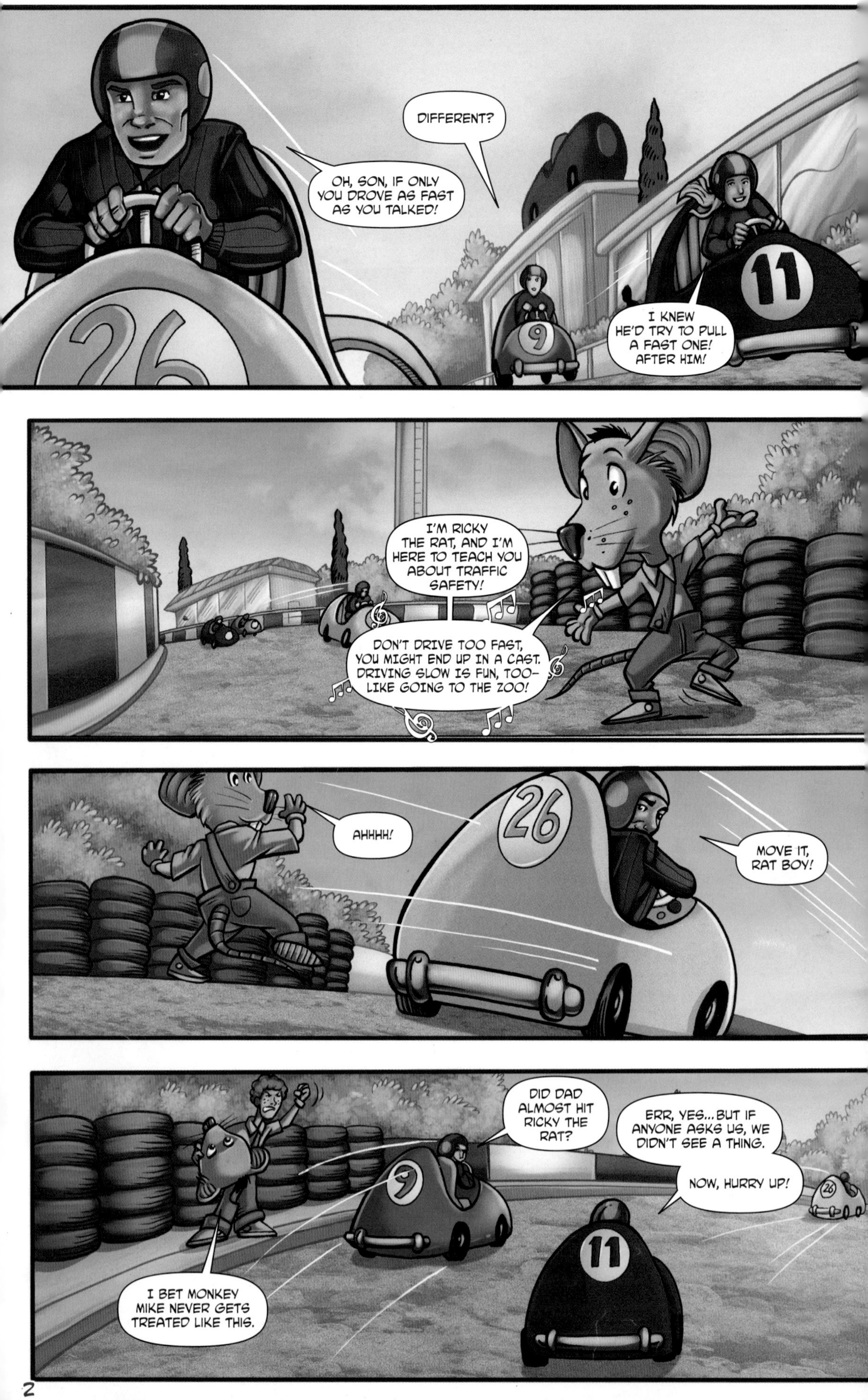

OH, SON, IF ONLY YOU DROVE AS FAST AS YOU TALKED!
DIFFERENT?
I KNEW HE'D TRY TO PULL A FAST ONE! AFTER HIM!
I'M RICKY THE RAT, AND I'M HERE TO TEACH YOU ABOUT TRAFFIC SAFETY!
DON'T DRIVE TOO FAST, YOU MIGHT END UP IN A CAST. DRIVING SLOW IS FUN, TOO— LIKE GOING TO THE ZOO!
AHHHH!
MOVE IT, RAT BOY!
DID DAD ALMOST HIT RICKY THE RAT?
ERR, YES... BUT IF ANYONE ASKS US, WE DIDN'T SEE A THING.
NOW, HURRY UP!
I BET MONKEY MIKE NEVER GETS TREATED LIKE THIS.

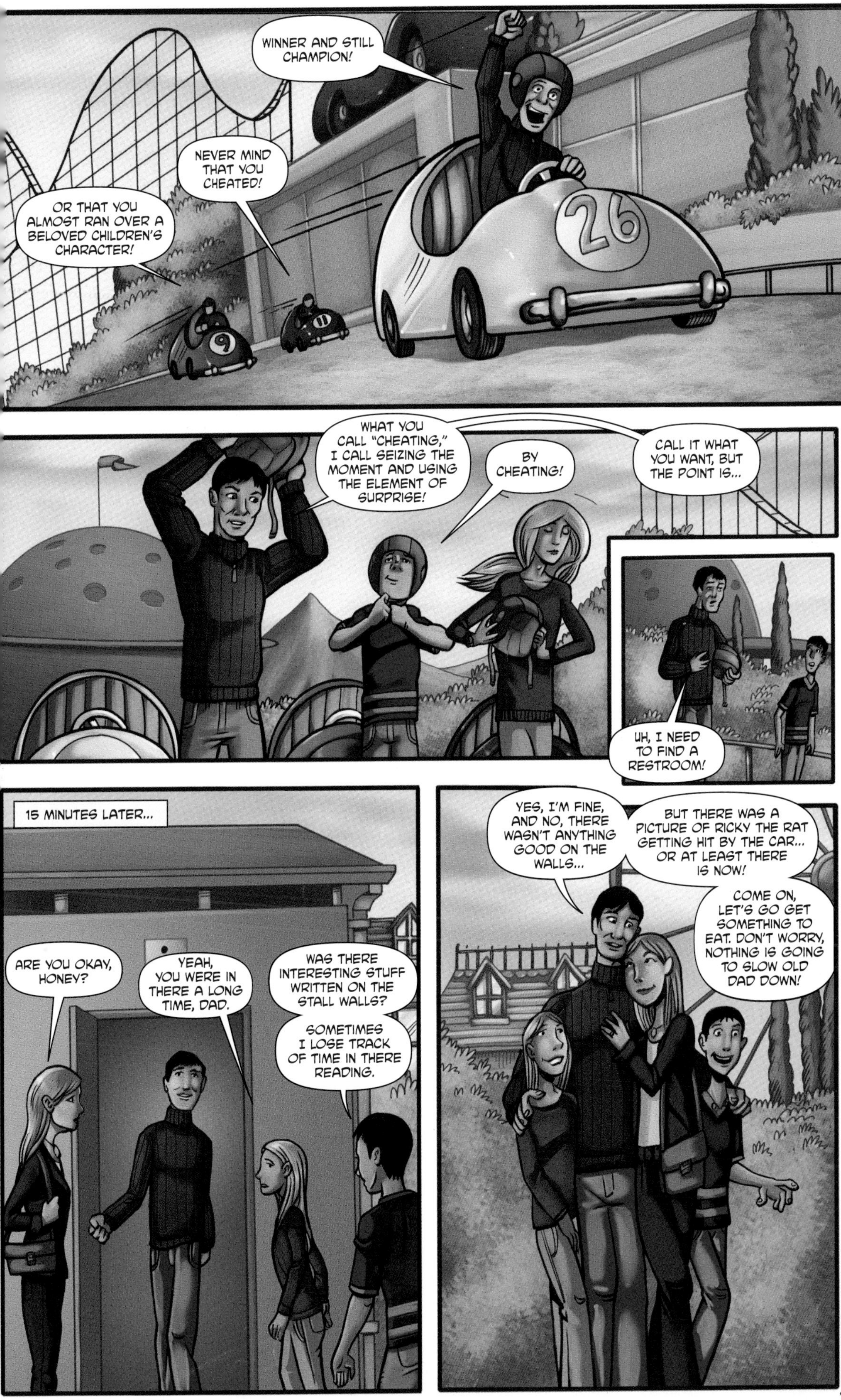
WINNER AND STILL CHAMPION!
NEVER MIND THAT YOU CHEATED!
OR THAT YOU ALMOST RAN OVER A BELOVED CHILDREN'S CHARACTER!
WHAT YOU CALL "CHEATING," I CALL SEIZING THE MOMENT AND USING THE ELEMENT OF SURPRISE!
BY CHEATING!
CALL IT WHAT YOU WANT, BUT THE POINT IS...
UH, I NEED TO FIND A RESTROOM!
15 MINUTES LATER...
ARE YOU OKAY, HONEY?
YEAH, YOU WERE IN THERE A LONG TIME, DAD.
WAS THERE INTERESTING STUFF WRITTEN ON THE STALL WALLS?
SOMETIMES I LOSE TRACK OF TIME IN THERE READING.
YES, I'M FINE, AND NO, THERE WASN'T ANYTHING GOOD ON THE WALLS...
BUT THERE WAS A PICTURE OF RICKY THE RAT GETTING HIT BY THE CAR... OR AT LEAST THERE IS NOW!
COME ON, LET'S GO GET SOMETHING TO EAT. DON'T WORRY, NOTHING IS GOING TO SLOW OLD DAD DOWN!

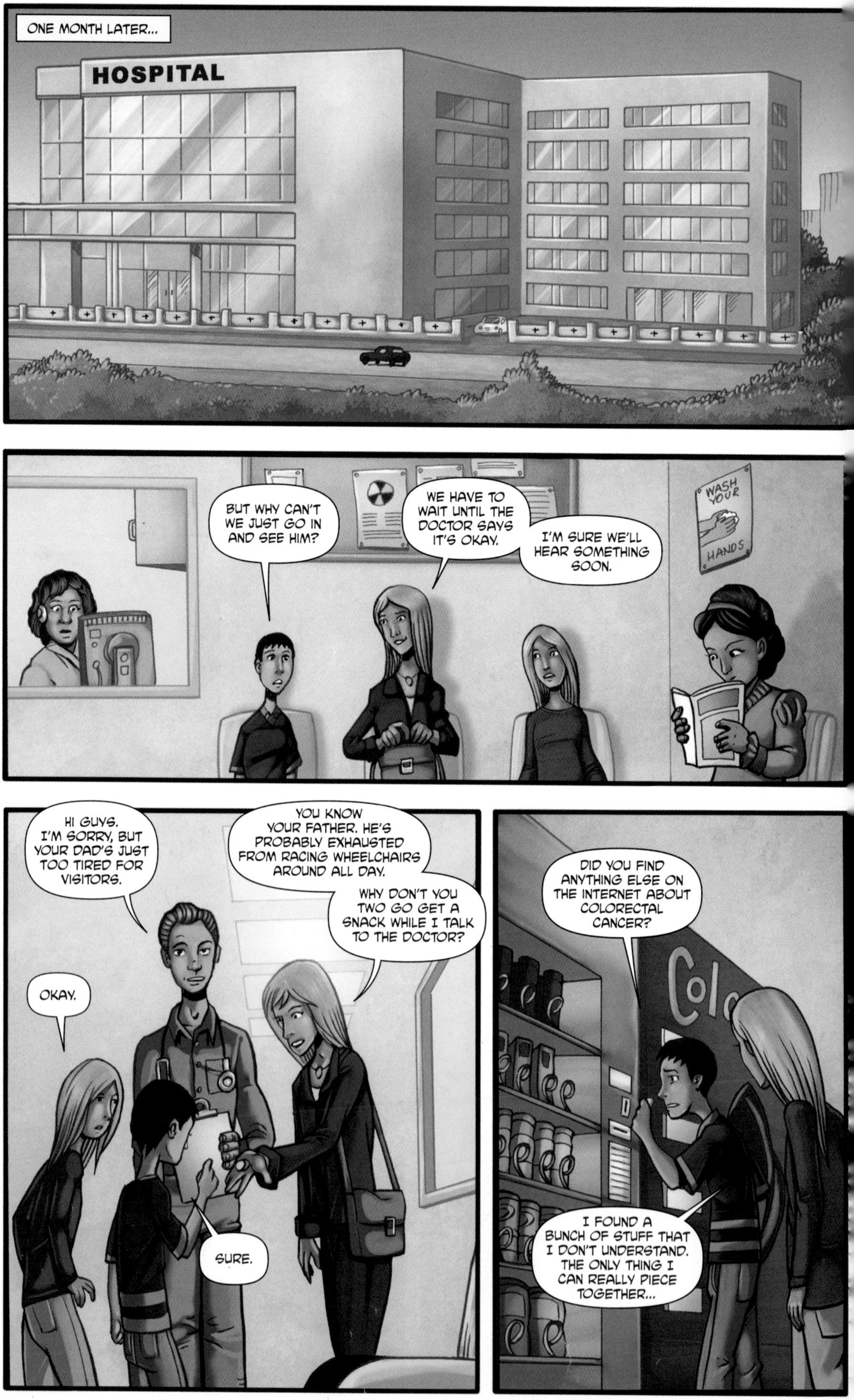
ONE MONTH LATER...
HOSPITAL
BUT WHY CAN'T WE JUST GO IN AND SEE HIM?
WE HAVE TO WAIT UNTIL THE DOCTOR SAYS IT'S OKAY.
I'M SURE WE'LL HEAR SOMETHING SOON.
WASH YOUR HANDS
HI GUYS. I'M SORRY, BUT YOUR DAD'S JUST TOO TIRED FOR VISITORS.
YOU KNOW YOUR FATHER. HE'S PROBABLY EXHAUSTED FROM RACING WHEELCHAIRS AROUND ALL DAY.
WHY DON'T YOU TWO GO GET A SNACK WHILE I TALK TO THE DOCTOR?
OKAY.
SURE.
DID YOU FIND ANYTHING ELSE ON THE INTERNET ABOUT COLORECTAL CANCER?
I FOUND A BUNCH OF STUFF THAT I DON'T UNDERSTAND. THE ONLY THING I CAN REALLY PIECE TOGETHER...

IS THAT IT'S BAD.

ALICE AND CHARLIE ARE HAVING A TOUGH TIME.

AGREED. THEY NEED HELP UNDERSTANDING THEIR FATHER'S COLORECTAL CANCER.

TELEPORTING NOW!

WHOA, WHAT THE...IT'S THE

MEDIKIDZ

IN THE AWESOMENESS... I MEAN FLESH. NAH, I MEAN AWESOMENESS.

NOTE TO SELF, WHEN YOU HIT THE BUTTON FOR CHIPS ON THE VENDING MACHINE, YOU ARE TRANSPORTED TO ANOTHER PLANET!

IT'S SCARY TO HEAR THAT SOMEONE YOU LOVE HAS *COLORECTAL CANCER*, BUT WE'RE GOING TO HELP YOU UNDERSTAND WHAT THAT MEANS BY TAKING YOU GUYS ON AN ADVENTURE THROUGH MEDILAND!

IF YOU WANT US TO BE CONSCIOUS FOR THE ADVENTURE, I'D LET GO!

ON THE PLUS SIDE, NOT BEING ABLE TO BREATHE MEANS WE CAN'T SMELL HIM.

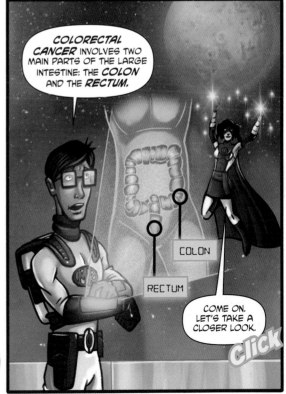

COLORECTAL CANCER INVOLVES TWO MAIN PARTS OF THE LARGE INTESTINE: THE *COLON* AND THE *RECTUM*.

COLON

RECTUM

COME ON. LET'S TAKE A CLOSER LOOK.

Click

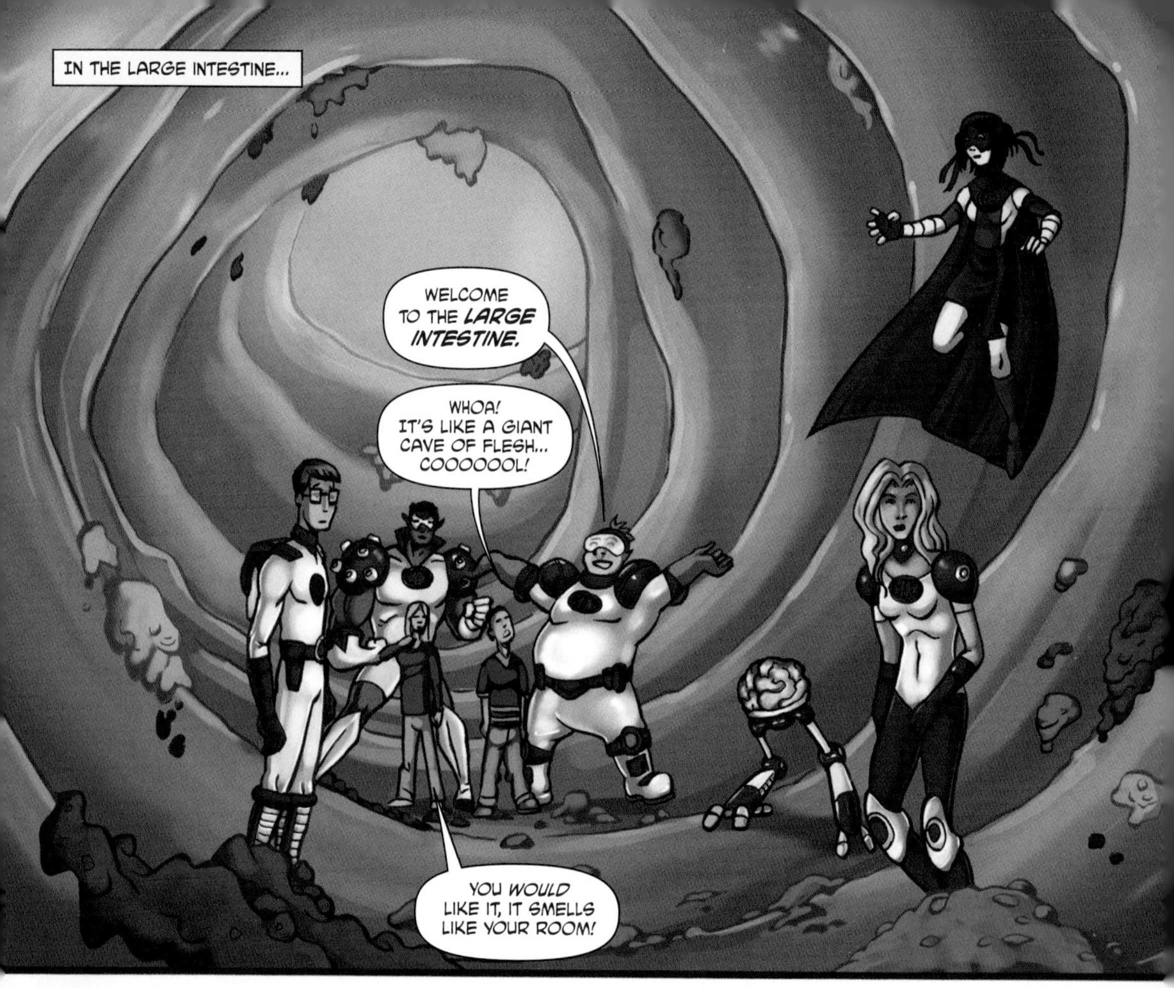
IN THE LARGE INTESTINE...
WELCOME TO THE **LARGE INTESTINE.**
WHOA! IT'S LIKE A GIANT CAVE OF FLESH... COOOOOOL!
YOU *WOULD* LIKE IT, IT SMELLS LIKE YOUR ROOM!

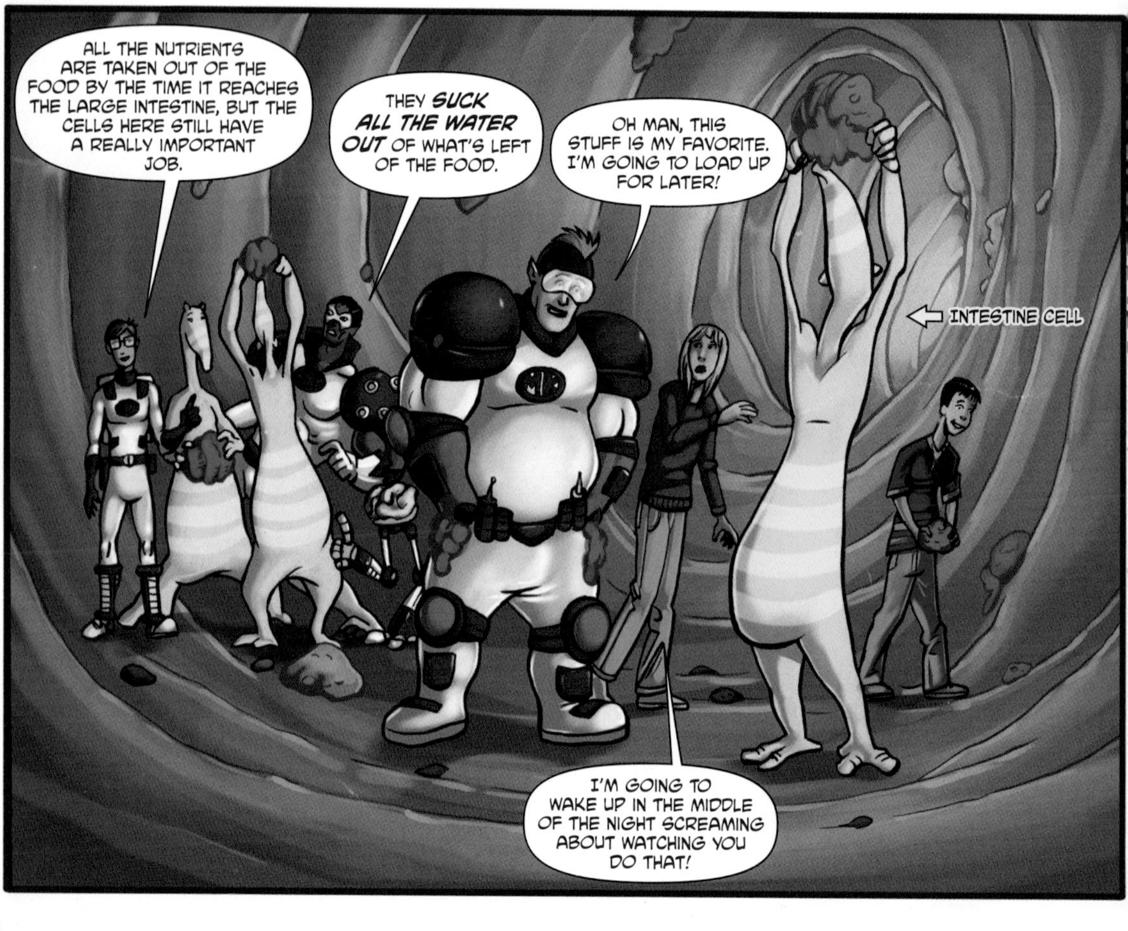
ALL THE NUTRIENTS ARE TAKEN OUT OF THE FOOD BY THE TIME IT REACHES THE LARGE INTESTINE, BUT THE CELLS HERE STILL HAVE A REALLY IMPORTANT JOB.
THEY **SUCK ALL THE WATER OUT** OF WHAT'S LEFT OF THE FOOD.
OH MAN, THIS STUFF IS MY FAVORITE. I'M GOING TO LOAD UP FOR LATER!
INTESTINE CELL
I'M GOING TO WAKE UP IN THE MIDDLE OF THE NIGHT SCREAMING ABOUT WATCHING YOU DO THAT!

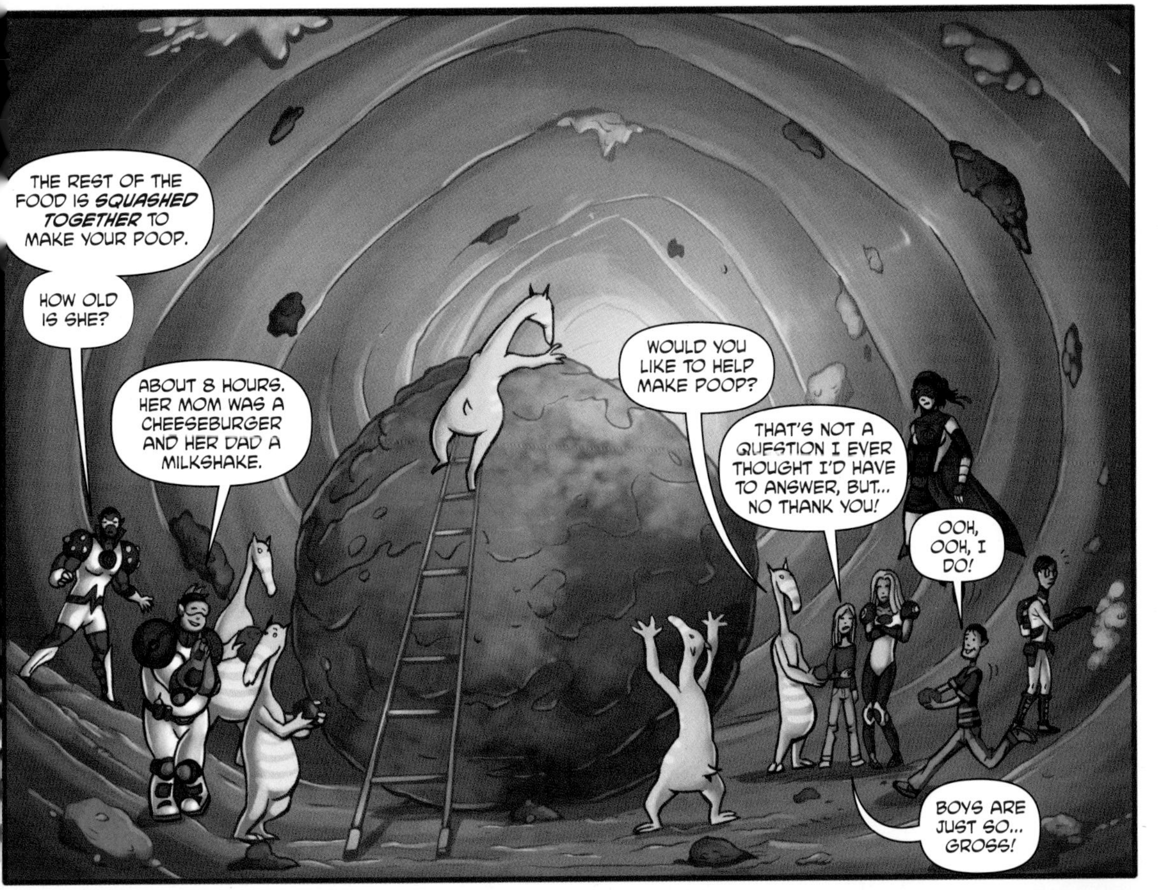
THE REST OF THE FOOD IS SQUASHED TOGETHER TO MAKE YOUR POOP.
HOW OLD IS SHE?
ABOUT 8 HOURS. HER MOM WAS A CHEESEBURGER AND HER DAD A MILKSHAKE.
WOULD YOU LIKE TO HELP MAKE POOP?
THAT'S NOT A QUESTION I EVER THOUGHT I'D HAVE TO ANSWER, BUT... NO THANK YOU!
OOH, OOH, I DO!
BOYS ARE JUST SO... GROSS!

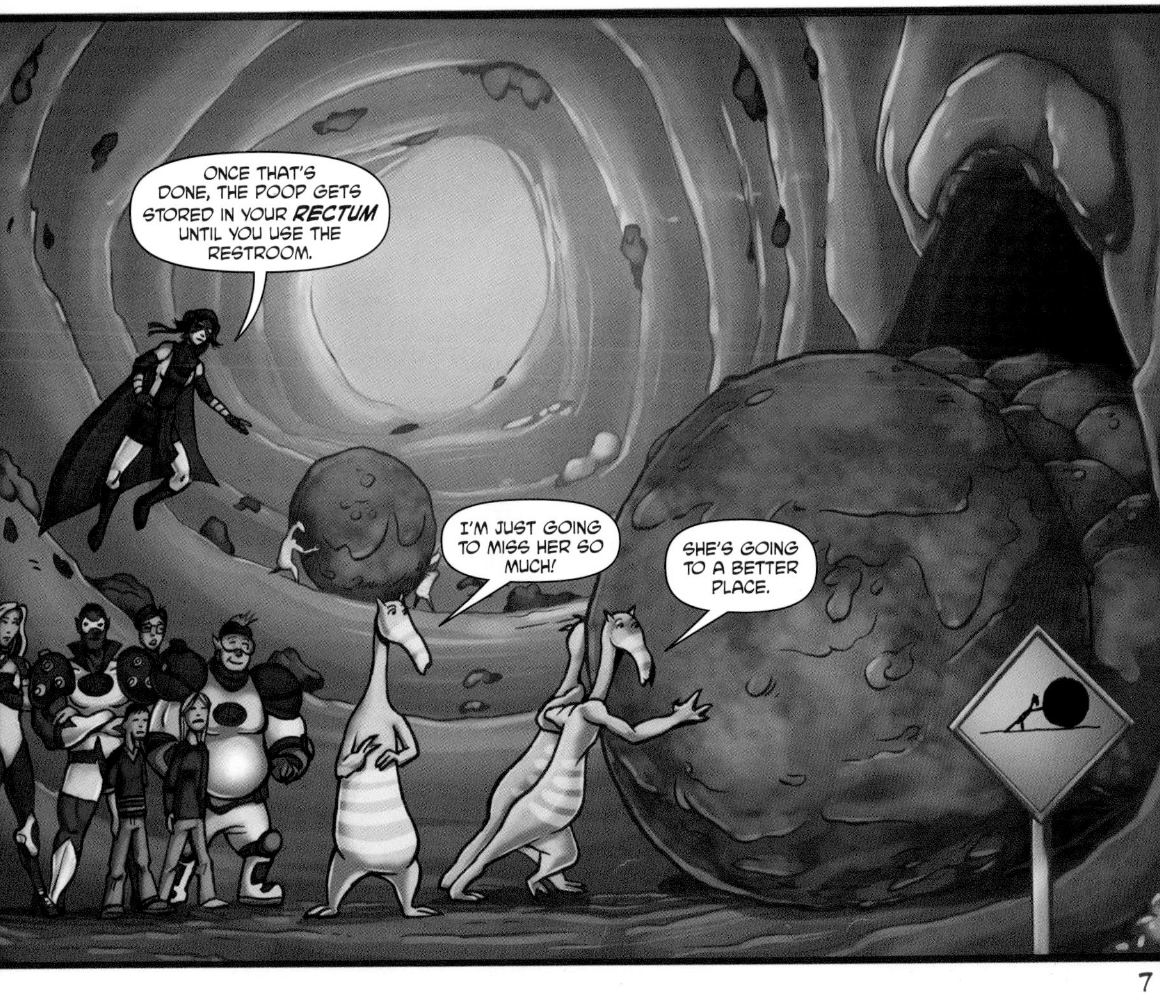
ONCE THAT'S DONE, THE POOP GETS STORED IN YOUR RECTUM UNTIL YOU USE THE RESTROOM.
I'M JUST GOING TO MISS HER SO MUCH!
SHE'S GOING TO A BETTER PLACE.

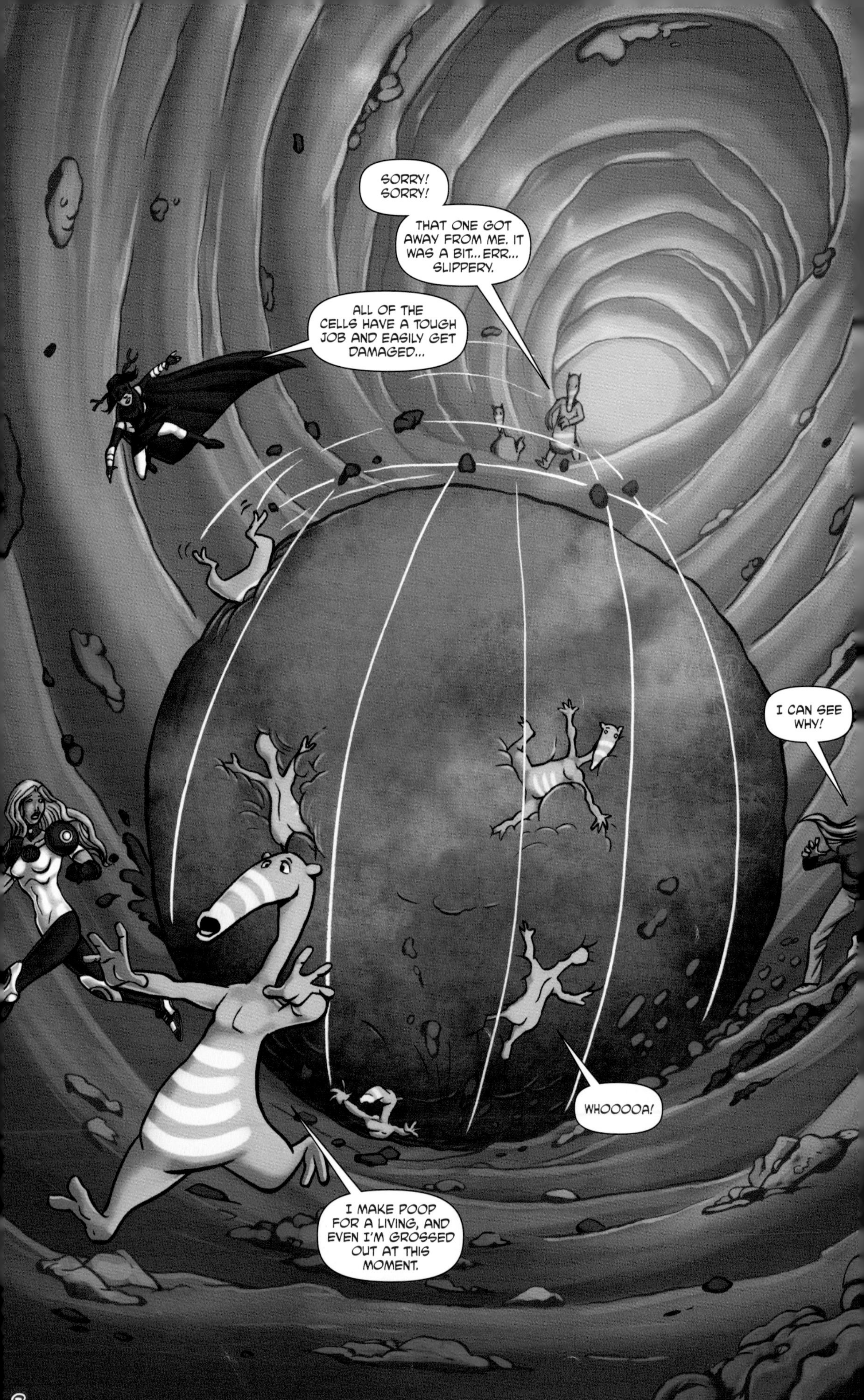
SORRY! SORRY!
THAT ONE GOT AWAY FROM ME. IT WAS A BIT... ERR... SLIPPERY.
ALL OF THE CELLS HAVE A TOUGH JOB AND EASILY GET DAMAGED...
I CAN SEE WHY!
WHOOOOA!
I MAKE POOP FOR A LIVING, AND EVEN I'M GROSSED OUT AT THIS MOMENT.

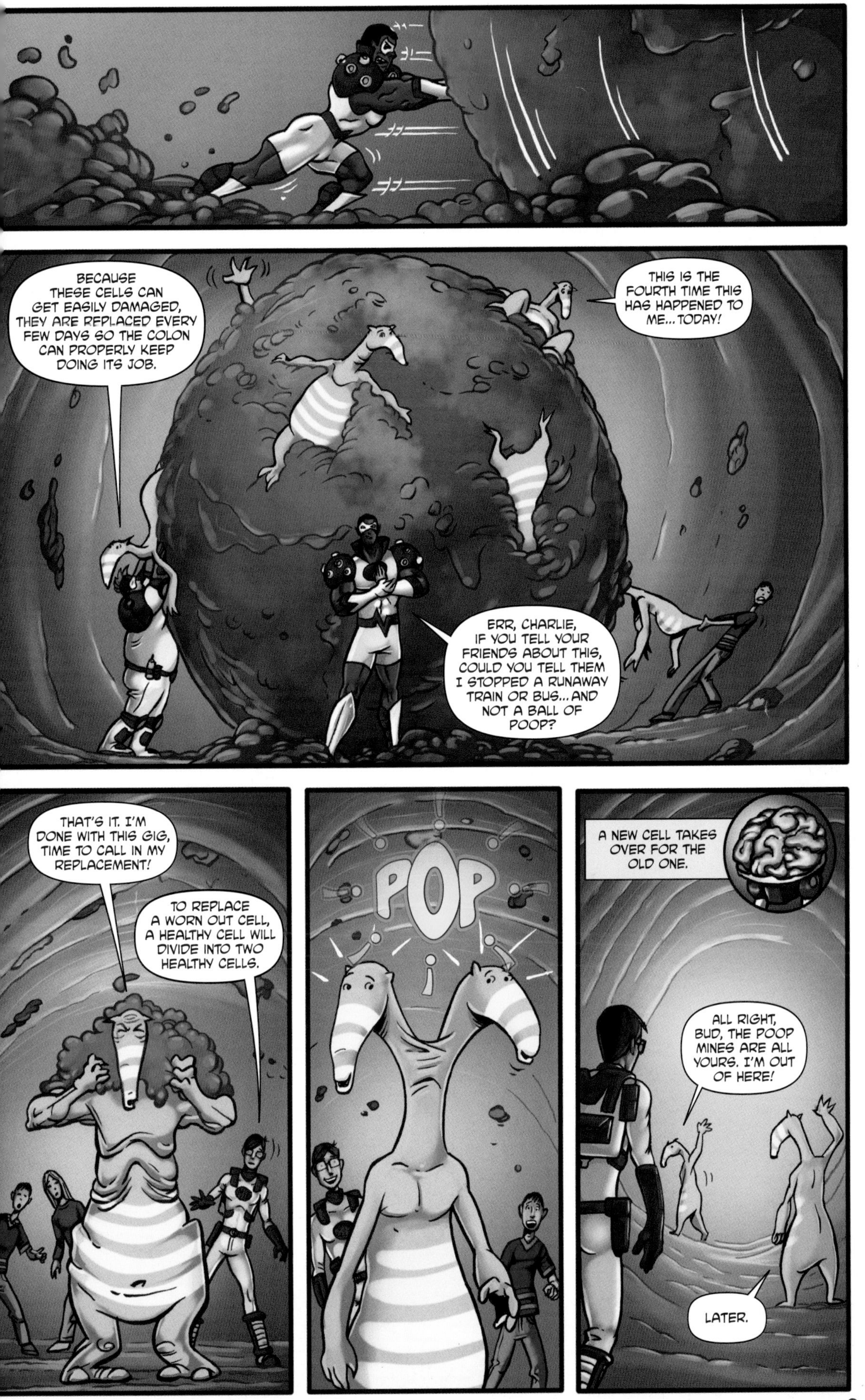
BECAUSE THESE CELLS CAN GET EASILY DAMAGED, THEY ARE REPLACED EVERY FEW DAYS SO THE COLON CAN PROPERLY KEEP DOING ITS JOB.
THIS IS THE FOURTH TIME THIS HAS HAPPENED TO ME... TODAY!
ERR, CHARLIE, IF YOU TELL YOUR FRIENDS ABOUT THIS, COULD YOU TELL THEM I STOPPED A RUNAWAY TRAIN OR BUS... AND NOT A BALL OF POOP?
THAT'S IT. I'M DONE WITH THIS GIG, TIME TO CALL IN MY REPLACEMENT!
TO REPLACE A WORN OUT CELL, A HEALTHY CELL WILL DIVIDE INTO TWO HEALTHY CELLS.
POP
A NEW CELL TAKES OVER FOR THE OLD ONE.
ALL RIGHT, BUD, THE POOP MINES ARE ALL YOURS. I'M OUT OF HERE!
LATER.

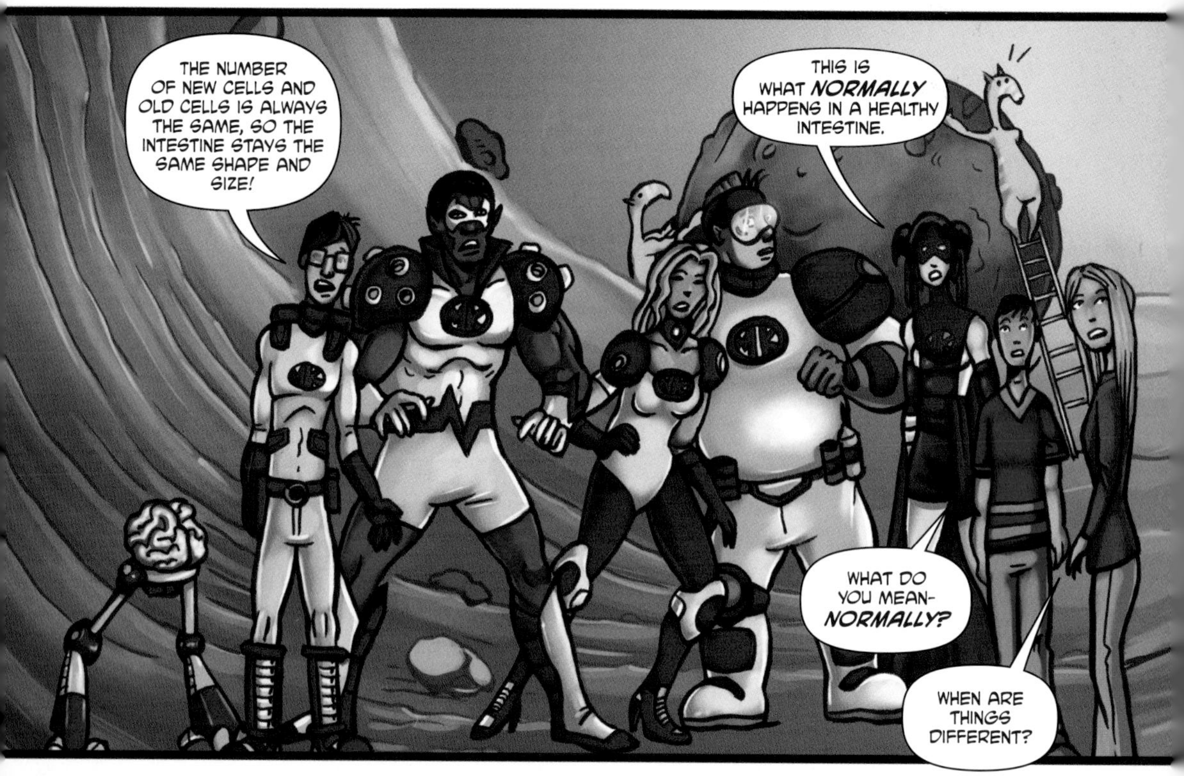
THE NUMBER OF NEW CELLS AND OLD CELLS IS ALWAYS THE SAME, SO THE INTESTINE STAYS THE SAME SHAPE AND SIZE!
THIS IS WHAT NORMALLY HAPPENS IN A HEALTHY INTESTINE.
WHAT DO YOU MEAN- NORMALLY?
WHEN ARE THINGS DIFFERENT?

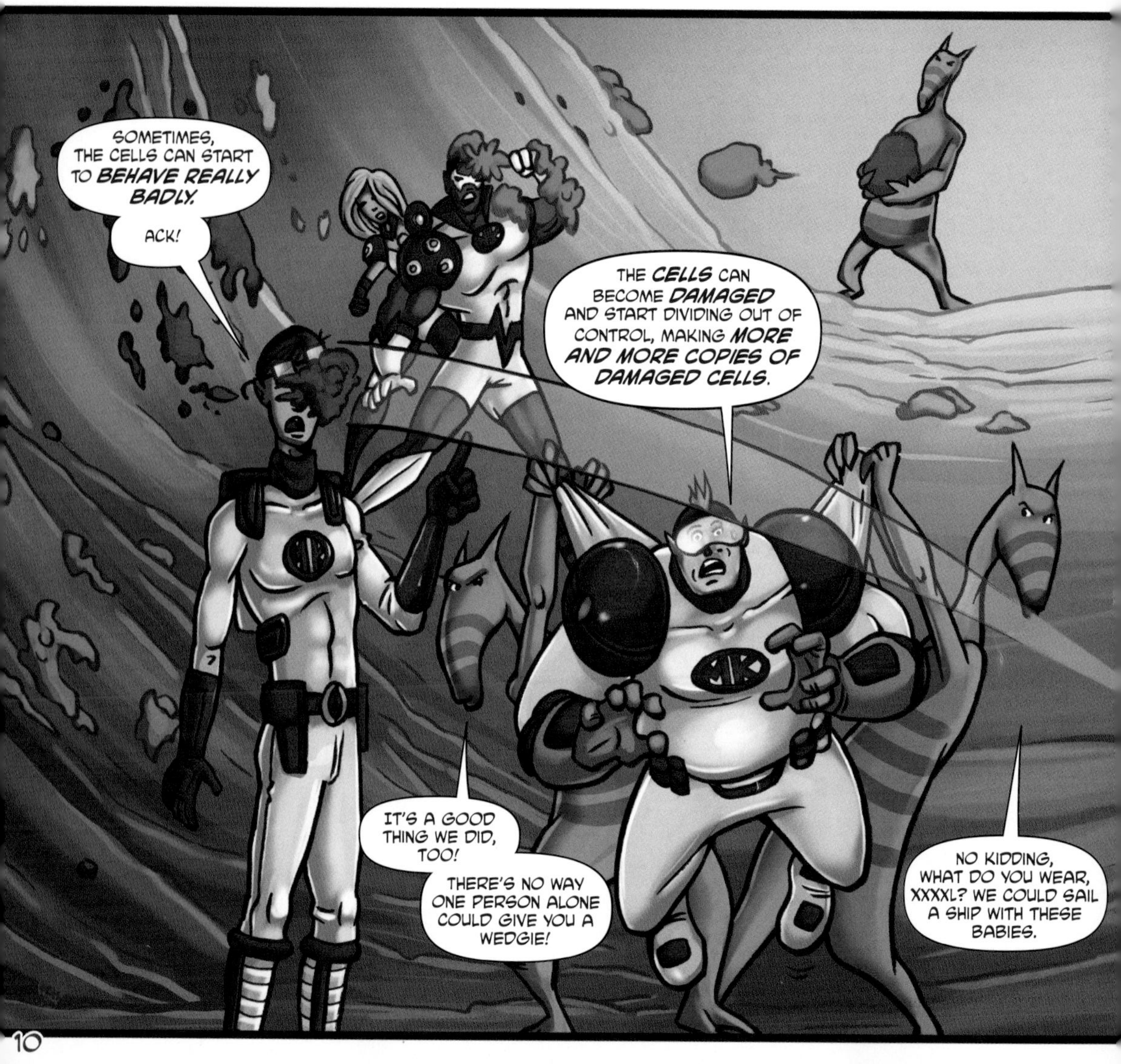
SOMETIMES, THE CELLS CAN START TO BEHAVE REALLY BADLY.
ACK!
THE CELLS CAN BECOME DAMAGED AND START DIVIDING OUT OF CONTROL, MAKING MORE AND MORE COPIES OF DAMAGED CELLS.
IT'S A GOOD THING WE DID, TOO!
THERE'S NO WAY ONE PERSON ALONE COULD GIVE YOU A WEDGIE!
NO KIDDING, WHAT DO YOU WEAR, XXXXL? WE COULD SAIL A SHIP WITH THESE BABIES.

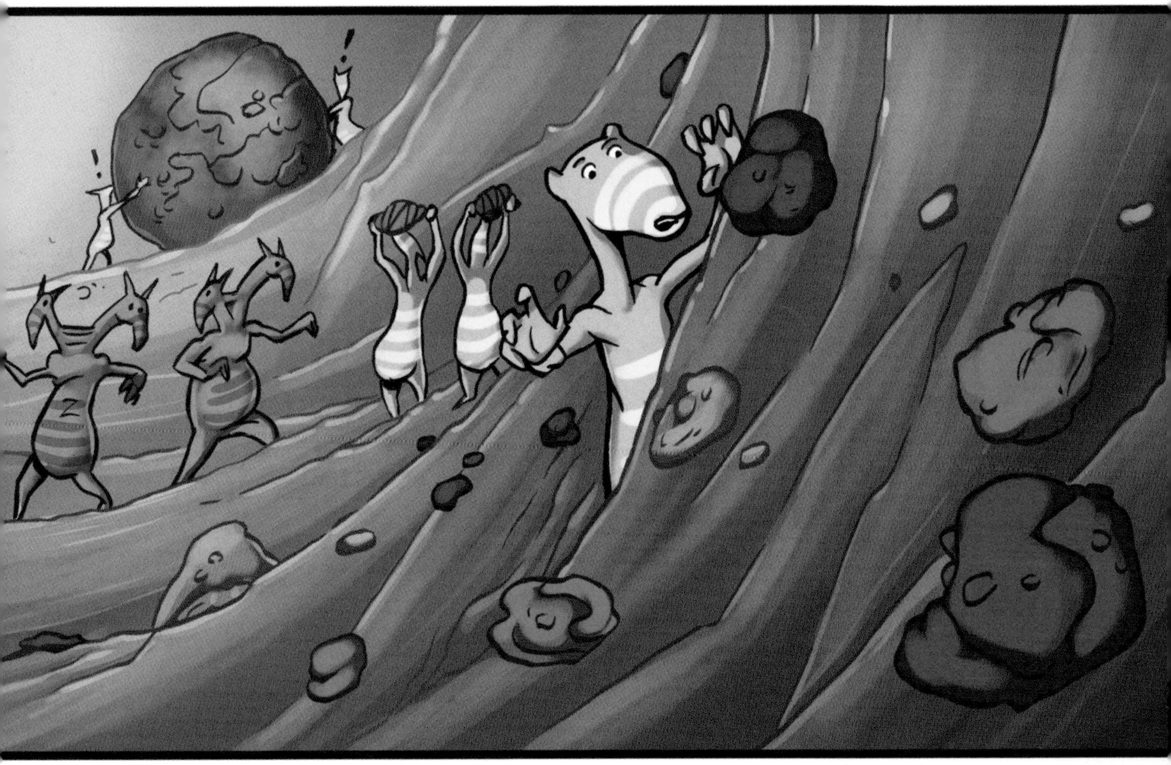

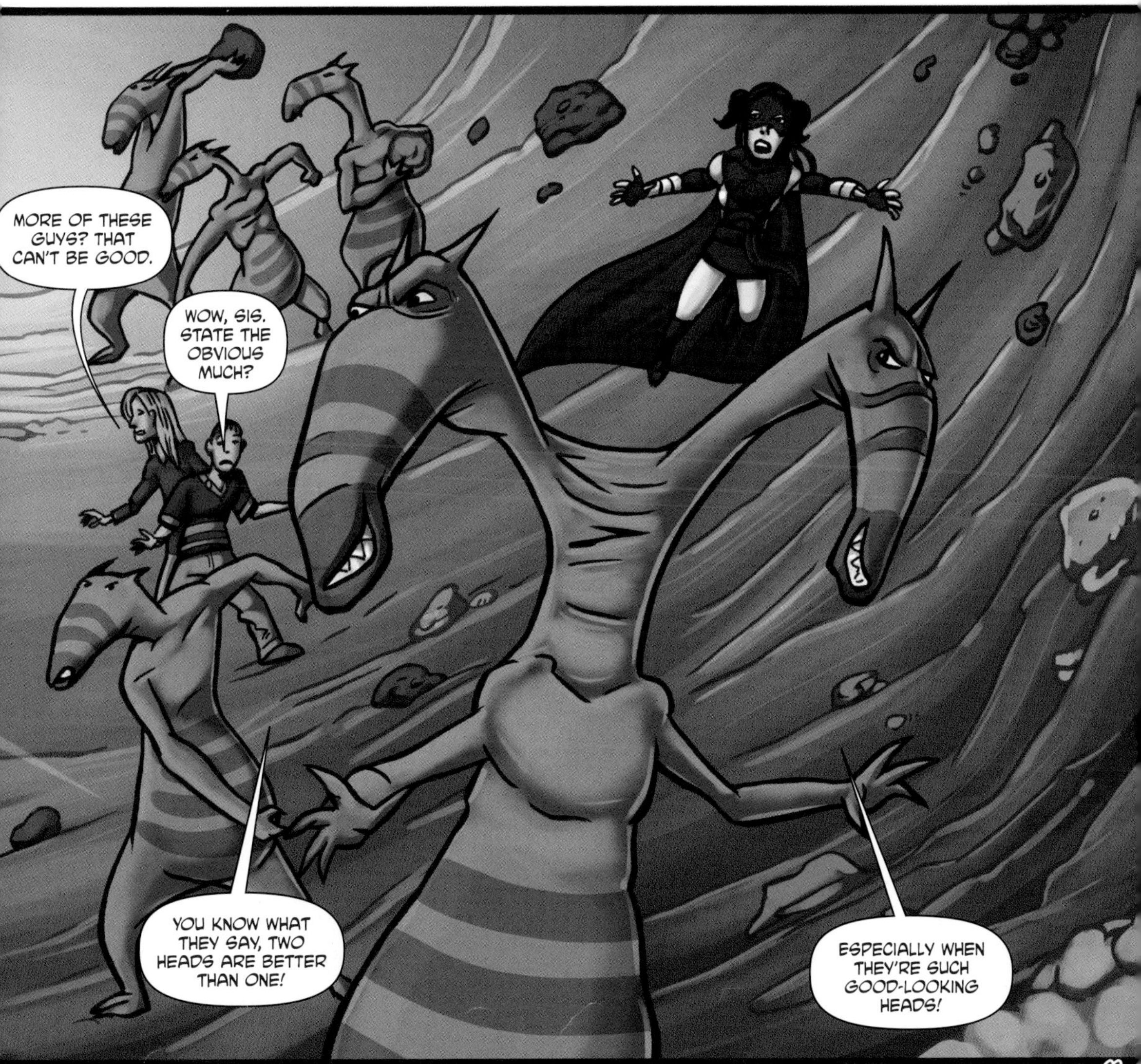

MORE OF THESE GUYS? THAT CAN'T BE GOOD.
WOW, SIS. STATE THE OBVIOUS MUCH?
YOU KNOW WHAT THEY SAY, TWO HEADS ARE BETTER THAN ONE!
ESPECIALLY WHEN THEY'RE SUCH GOOD-LOOKING HEADS!

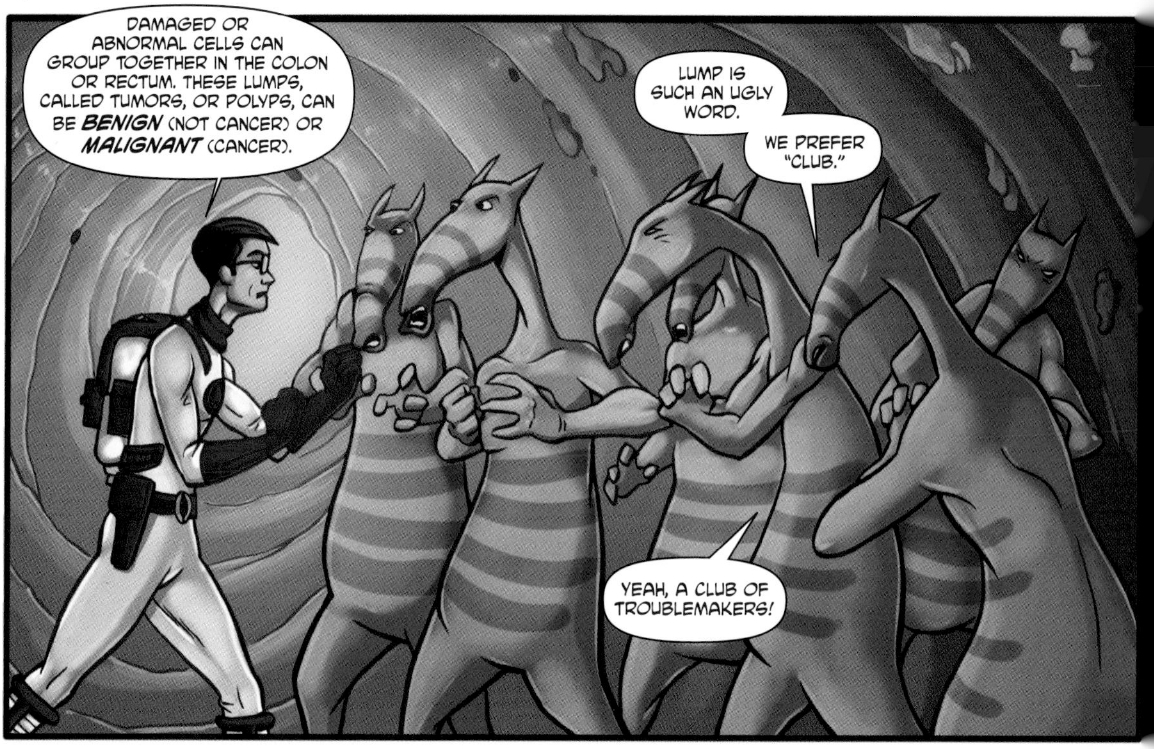
DAMAGED OR ABNORMAL CELLS CAN GROUP TOGETHER IN THE COLON OR RECTUM. THESE LUMPS, CALLED TUMORS, OR POLYPS, CAN BE **BENIGN** (NOT CANCER) OR **MALIGNANT** (CANCER).
LUMP IS SUCH AN UGLY WORD.
WE PREFER "CLUB."
YEAH, A CLUB OF TROUBLEMAKERS!

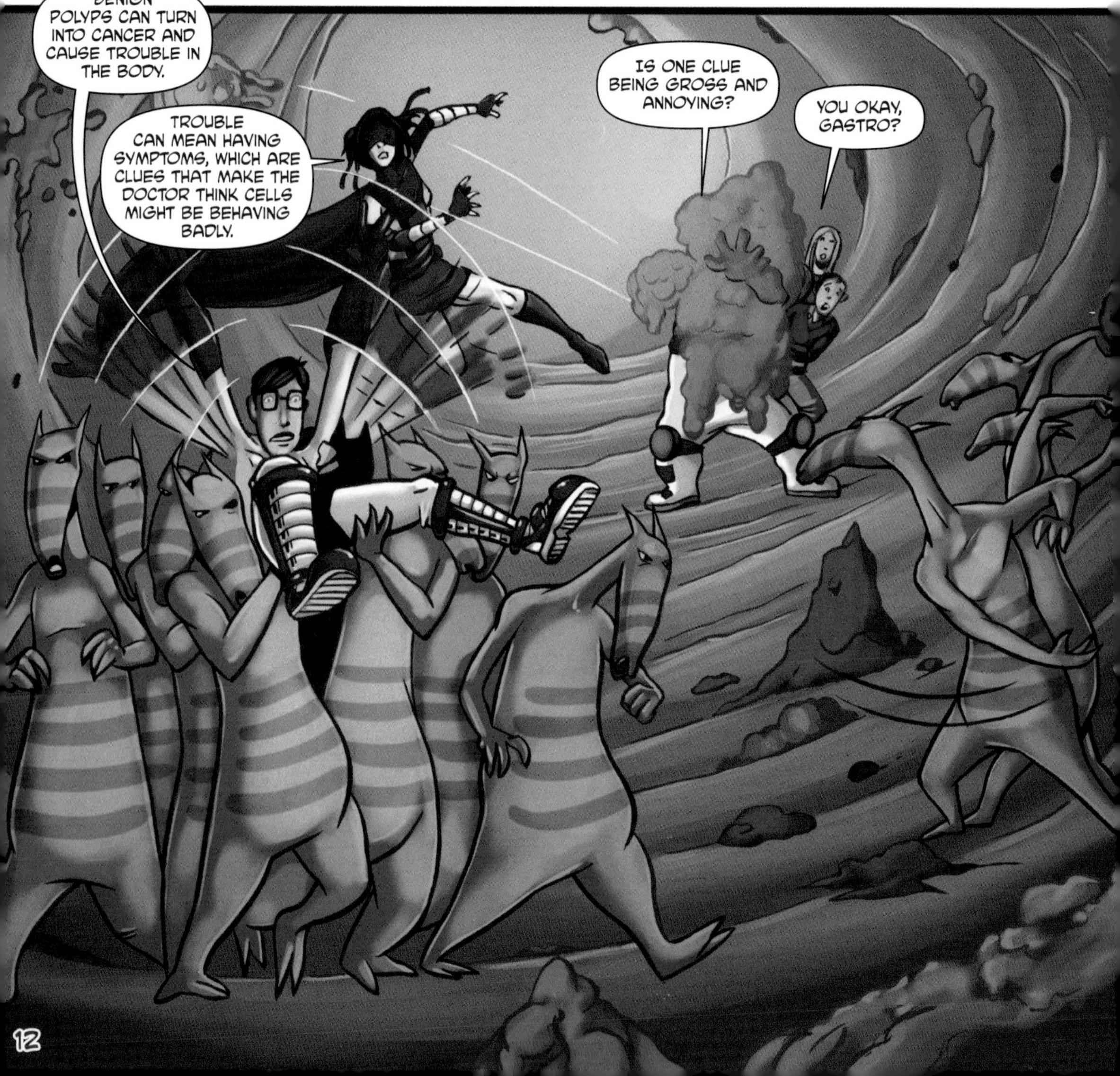
BENIGN POLYPS CAN TURN INTO CANCER AND CAUSE TROUBLE IN THE BODY.
TROUBLE CAN MEAN HAVING SYMPTOMS, WHICH ARE CLUES THAT MAKE THE DOCTOR THINK CELLS MIGHT BE BEHAVING BADLY.
IS ONE CLUE BEING GROSS AND ANNOYING?
YOU OKAY, GASTRO?

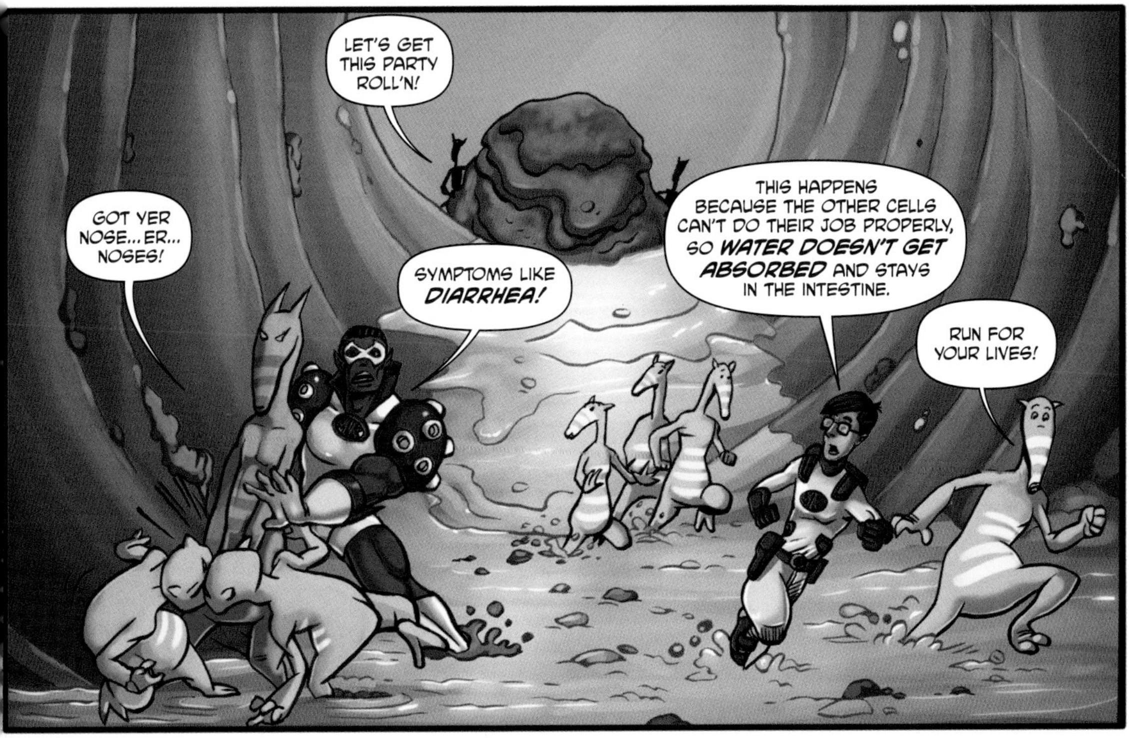
LET'S GET THIS PARTY ROLL'N!
GOT YER NOSE...ER... NOSES!
SYMPTOMS LIKE **DIARRHEA!**
THIS HAPPENS BECAUSE THE OTHER CELLS CAN'T DO THEIR JOB PROPERLY, SO **WATER DOESN'T GET ABSORBED** AND STAYS IN THE INTESTINE.
RUN FOR YOUR LIVES!

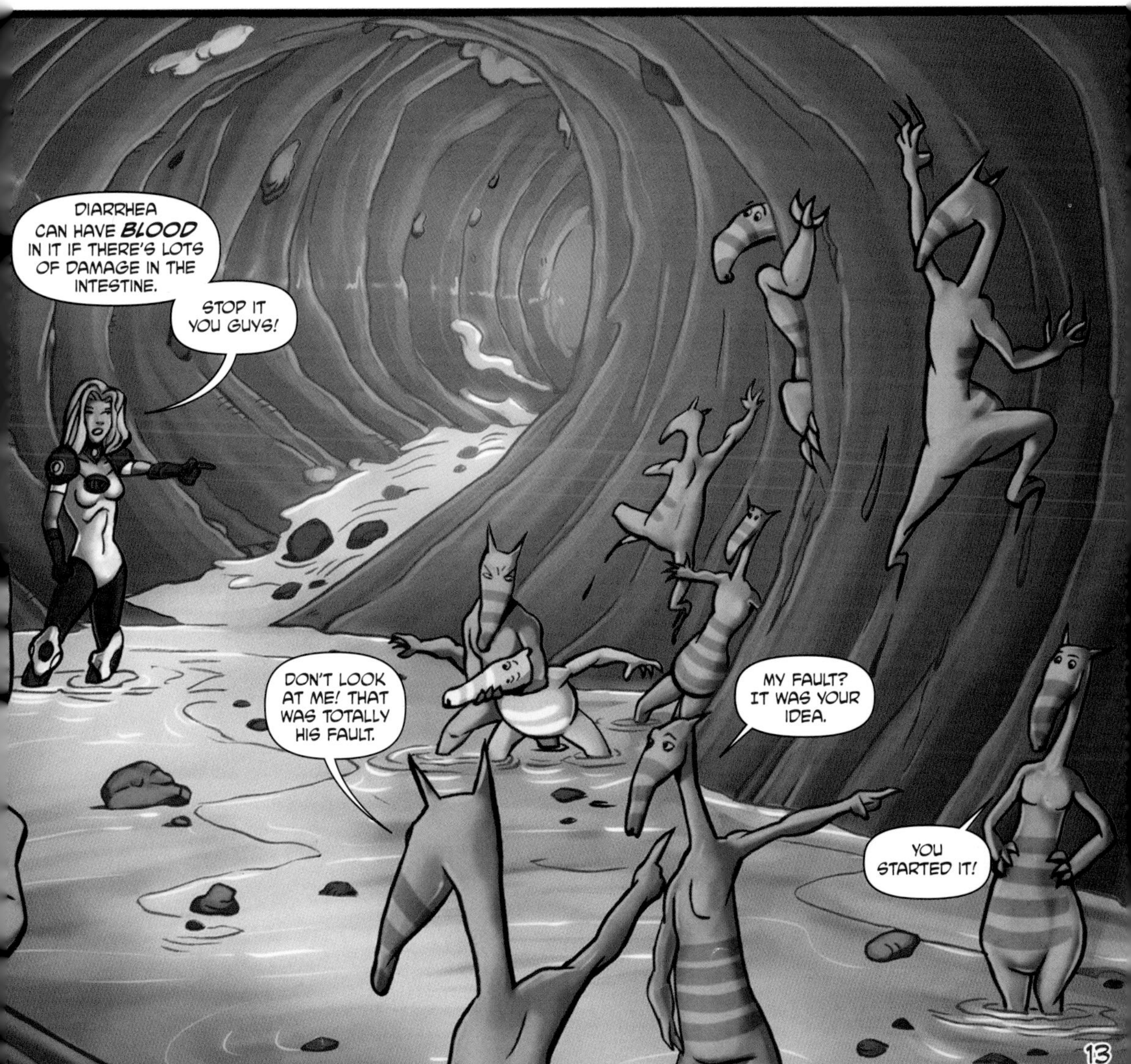
DIARRHEA CAN HAVE **BLOOD** IN IT IF THERE'S LOTS OF DAMAGE IN THE INTESTINE.
STOP IT YOU GUYS!
DON'T LOOK AT ME! THAT WAS TOTALLY HIS FAULT.
MY FAULT? IT WAS YOUR IDEA.
YOU STARTED IT!

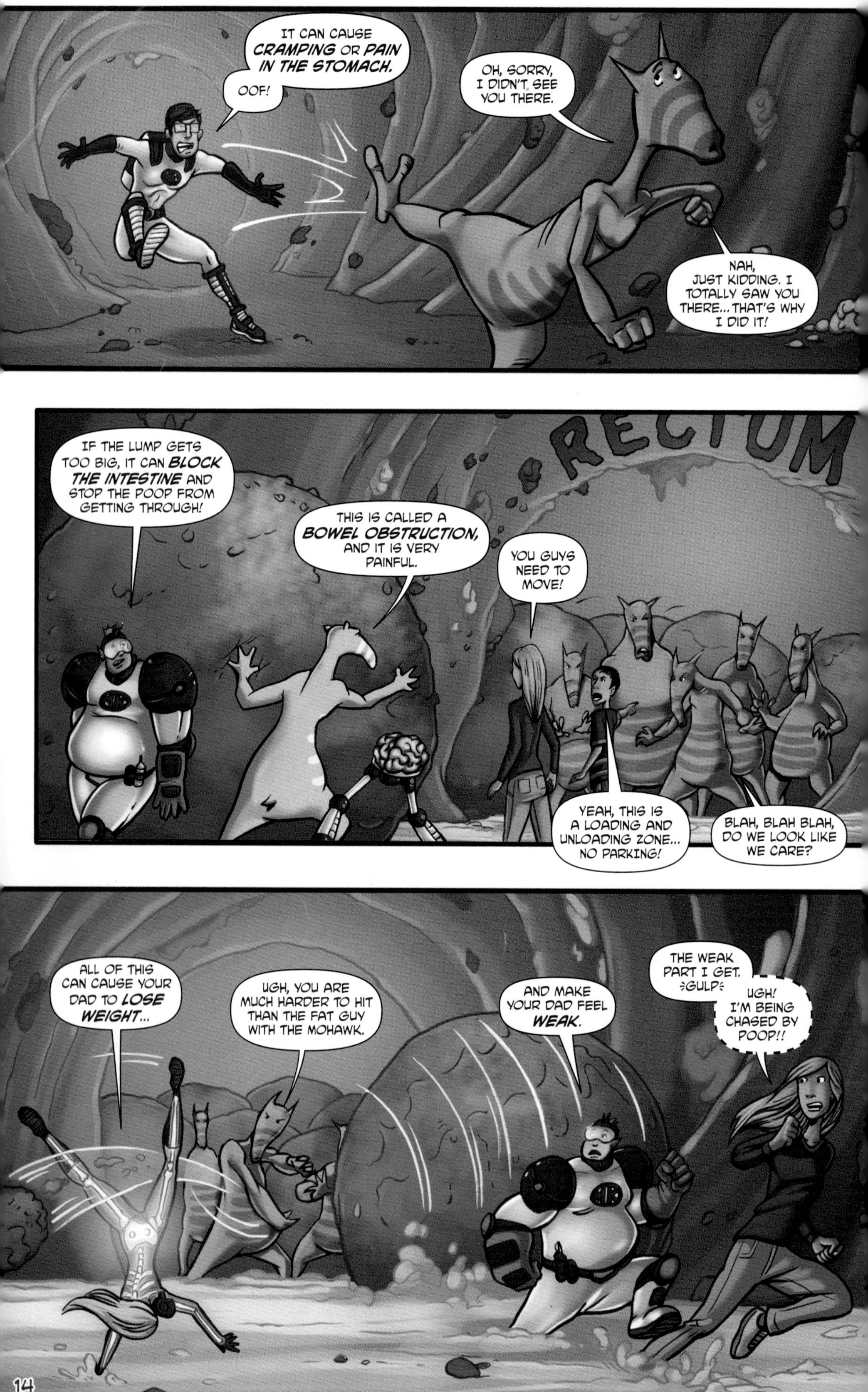
IT CAN CAUSE CRAMPING OR PAIN IN THE STOMACH.
OOF!
OH, SORRY, I DIDN'T SEE YOU THERE.
NAH, JUST KIDDING. I TOTALLY SAW YOU THERE...THAT'S WHY I DID IT!
RECTUM
IF THE LUMP GETS TOO BIG, IT CAN BLOCK THE INTESTINE AND STOP THE POOP FROM GETTING THROUGH!
THIS IS CALLED A BOWEL OBSTRUCTION, AND IT IS VERY PAINFUL.
YOU GUYS NEED TO MOVE!
YEAH, THIS IS A LOADING AND UNLOADING ZONE... NO PARKING!
BLAH, BLAH BLAH, DO WE LOOK LIKE WE CARE?
ALL OF THIS CAN CAUSE YOUR DAD TO LOSE WEIGHT...
UGH, YOU ARE MUCH HARDER TO HIT THAN THE FAT GUY WITH THE MOHAWK.
AND MAKE YOUR DAD FEEL WEAK.
THE WEAK PART I GET. ≶GULP≶
UGH! I'M BEING CHASED BY POOP!!

THESE SYMPTOMS MAY MAKE THE DOCTOR THINK THERE IS A TUMOR, BUT THE DOCTOR WILL HAVE TO RUN SOME *TESTS* TO BE CERTAIN.

ERR... WHAT ARE YOU PLANNING ON DOING WITH THAT?

NOTHING THAT INVOLVES YOU...

PHEW!

YET.

FIRST UP IS A *BLOOD TEST.*

A BLOOD TEST CAN RULE OUT OTHER PROBLEMS, SUCH AS INFECTIONS.

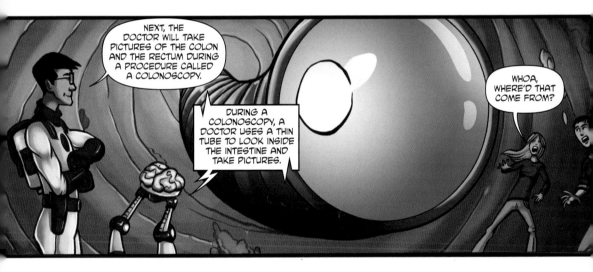

NEXT, THE DOCTOR WILL TAKE PICTURES OF THE COLON AND THE RECTUM DURING A PROCEDURE CALLED A COLONOSCOPY.

DURING A COLONOSCOPY, A DOCTOR USES A THIN TUBE TO LOOK INSIDE THE INTESTINE AND TAKE PICTURES.

WHOA, WHERE'D THAT COME FROM?

THE TUBE HAS A LIGHT AND A CAMERA ON THE END SO THE DOCTOR CAN *LITERALLY SEE* ANY POLYPS OR OTHER ABNORMAL GROWTHS IN THE LINING OF THE INTESTINE.

HEY, DO YOU MIND? WE'RE TRYING TO LURK HERE!

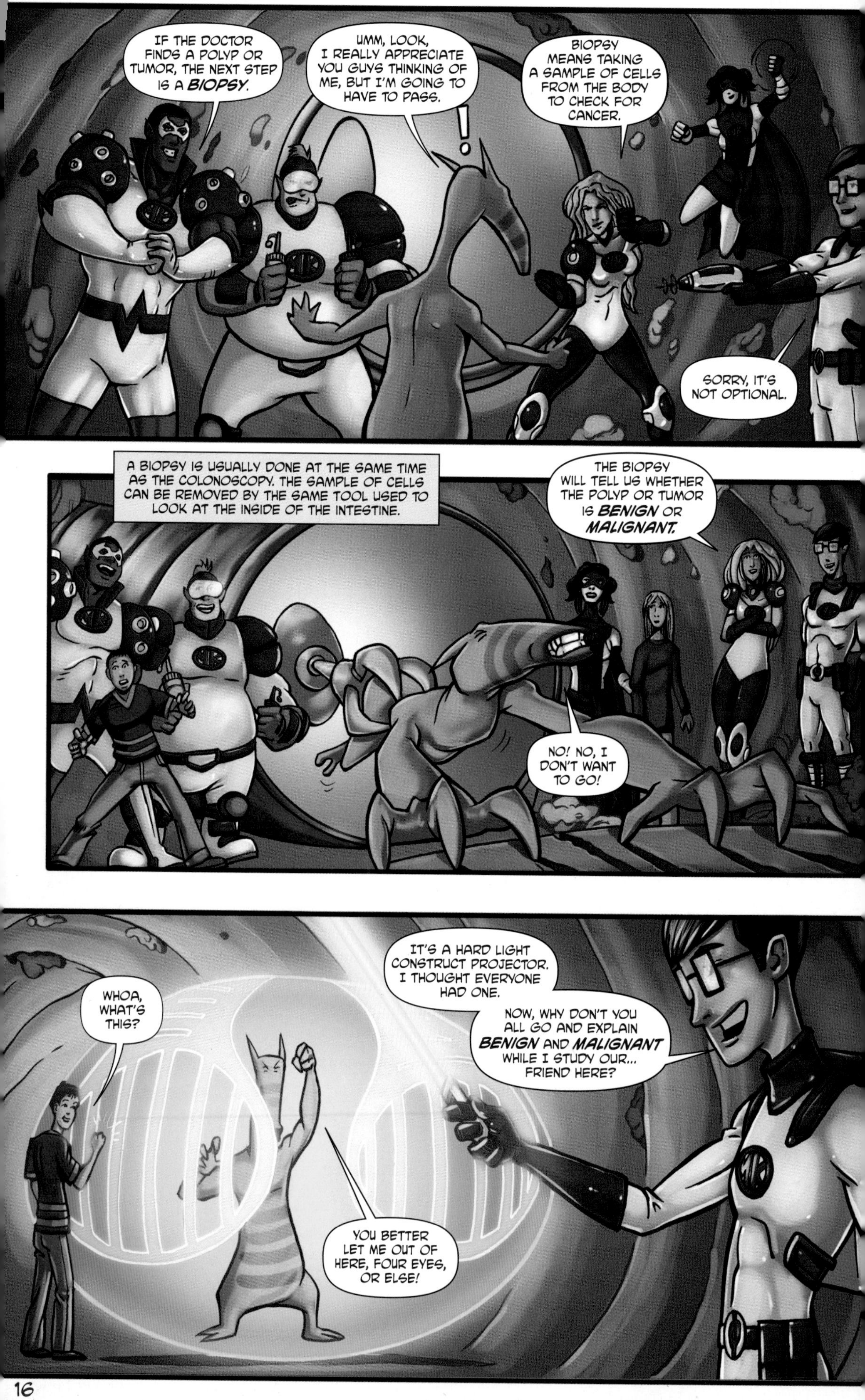
IF THE DOCTOR FINDS A POLYP OR TUMOR, THE NEXT STEP IS A ***BIOPSY***.
UMM, LOOK, I REALLY APPRECIATE YOU GUYS THINKING OF ME, BUT I'M GOING TO HAVE TO PASS.
!
BIOPSY MEANS TAKING A SAMPLE OF CELLS FROM THE BODY TO CHECK FOR CANCER.
SORRY, IT'S NOT OPTIONAL.
A BIOPSY IS USUALLY DONE AT THE SAME TIME AS THE COLONOSCOPY. THE SAMPLE OF CELLS CAN BE REMOVED BY THE SAME TOOL USED TO LOOK AT THE INSIDE OF THE INTESTINE.
THE BIOPSY WILL TELL US WHETHER THE POLYP OR TUMOR IS ***BENIGN*** OR ***MALIGNANT.***
NO! NO, I DON'T WANT TO GO!
WHOA, WHAT'S THIS?
IT'S A HARD LIGHT CONSTRUCT PROJECTOR. I THOUGHT EVERYONE HAD ONE.
NOW, WHY DON'T YOU ALL GO AND EXPLAIN ***BENIGN*** AND ***MALIGNANT*** WHILE I STUDY OUR... FRIEND HERE?
YOU BETTER LET ME OUT OF HERE, FOUR EYES, OR ELSE!

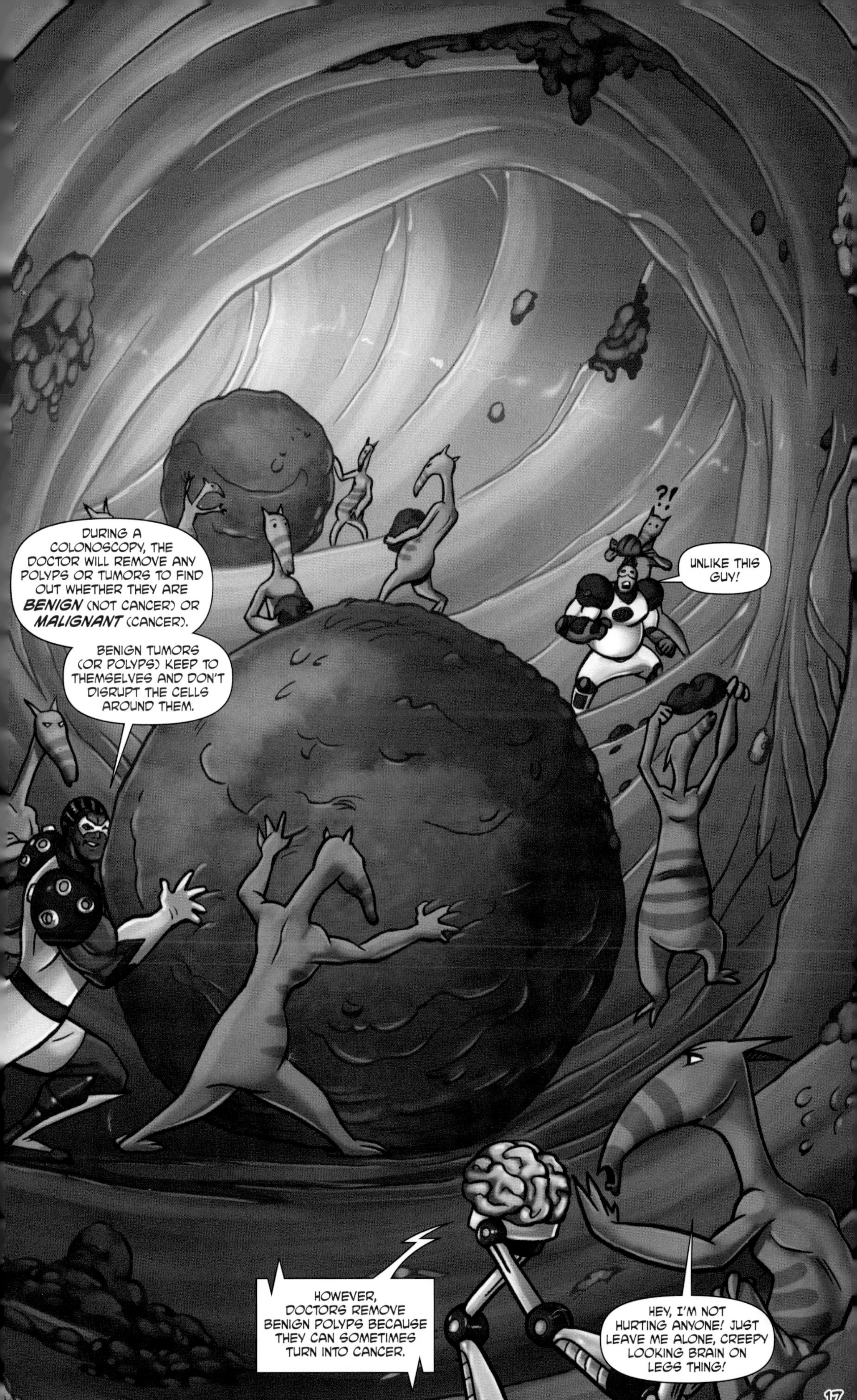
DURING A COLONOSCOPY, THE DOCTOR WILL REMOVE ANY POLYPS OR TUMORS TO FIND OUT WHETHER THEY ARE **BENIGN** (NOT CANCER) OR **MALIGNANT** (CANCER).
BENIGN TUMORS (OR POLYPS) KEEP TO THEMSELVES AND DON'T DISRUPT THE CELLS AROUND THEM.
?!
UNLIKE THIS GUY!
HOWEVER, DOCTORS REMOVE BENIGN POLYPS BECAUSE THEY CAN SOMETIMES TURN INTO CANCER.
HEY, I'M NOT HURTING ANYONE! JUST LEAVE ME ALONE, CREEPY LOOKING BRAIN ON LEGS THING!

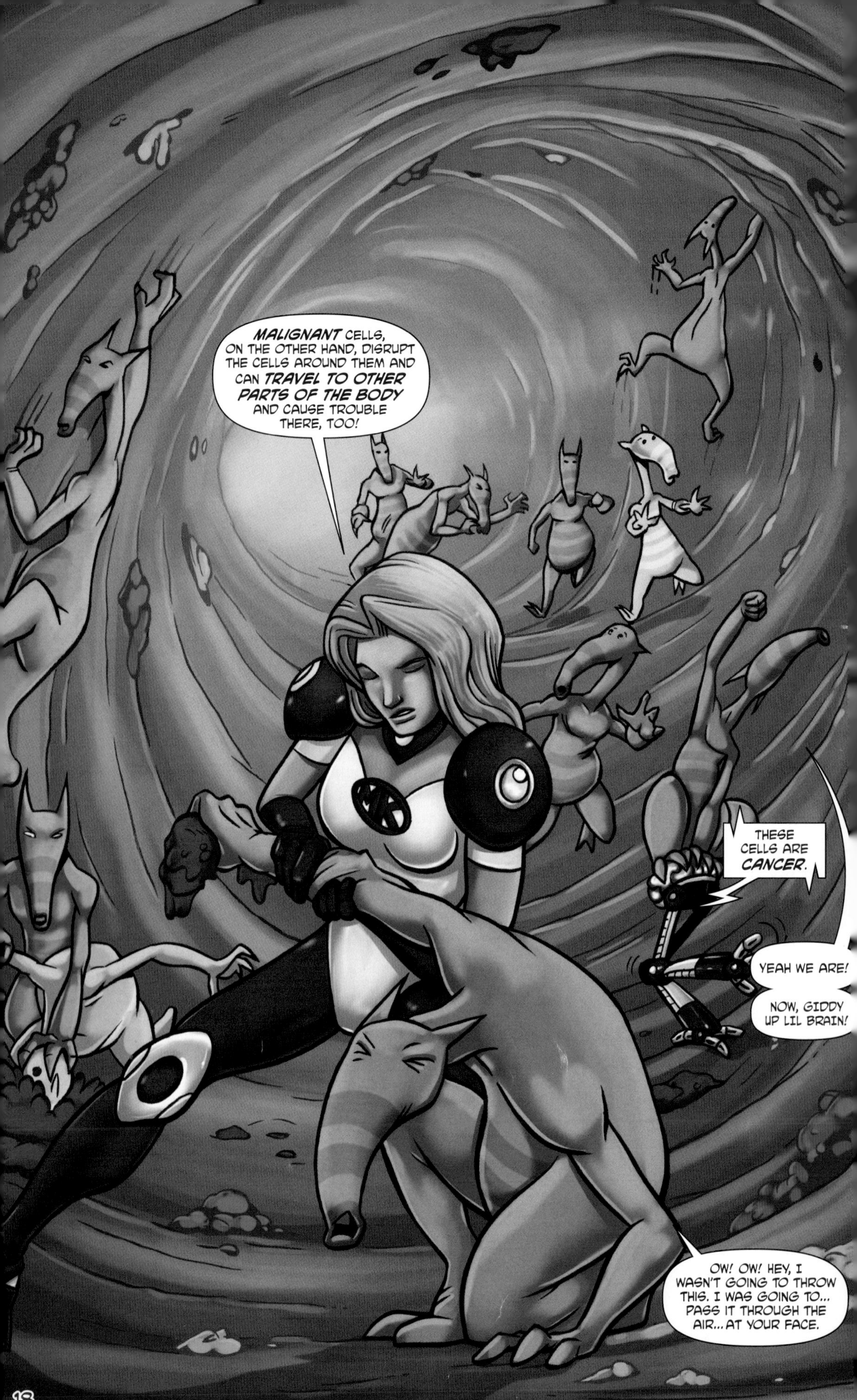
MALIGNANT CELLS, ON THE OTHER HAND, DISRUPT THE CELLS AROUND THEM AND CAN TRAVEL TO OTHER PARTS OF THE BODY AND CAUSE TROUBLE THERE, TOO!
THESE CELLS ARE CANCER.
YEAH WE ARE!
NOW, GIDDY UP LIL BRAIN!
OW! OW! HEY, I WASN'T GOING TO THROW THIS. I WAS GOING TO... PASS IT THROUGH THE AIR... AT YOUR FACE.

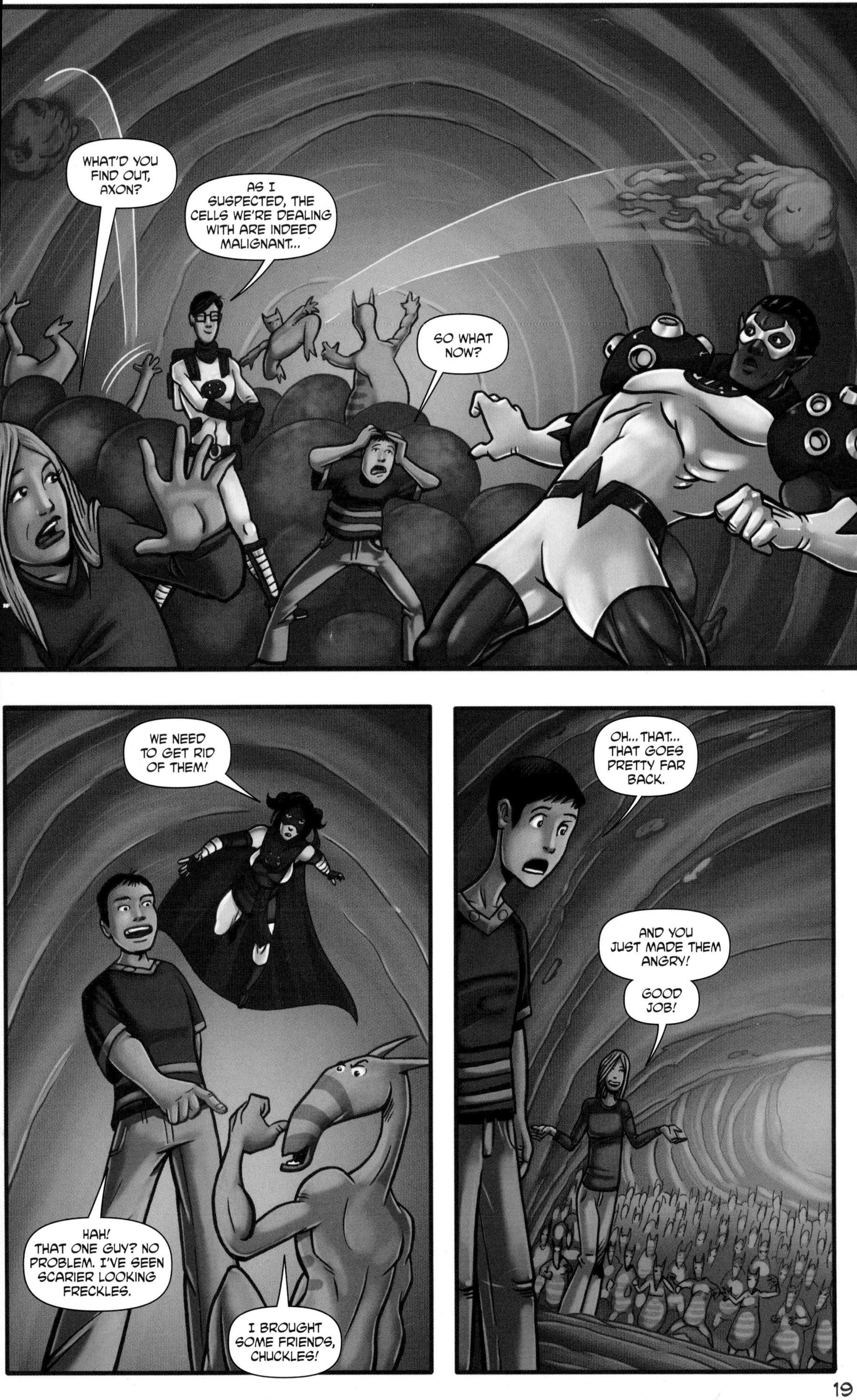
WHAT'D YOU FIND OUT, AXON?
AS I SUSPECTED, THE CELLS WE'RE DEALING WITH ARE INDEED MALIGNANT...
SO WHAT NOW?
WE NEED TO GET RID OF THEM!
HAH! THAT ONE GUY? NO PROBLEM. I'VE SEEN SCARIER LOOKING FRECKLES.
I BROUGHT SOME FRIENDS, CHUCKLES!
OH... THAT... THAT GOES PRETTY FAR BACK.
AND YOU JUST MADE THEM ANGRY!
GOOD JOB!

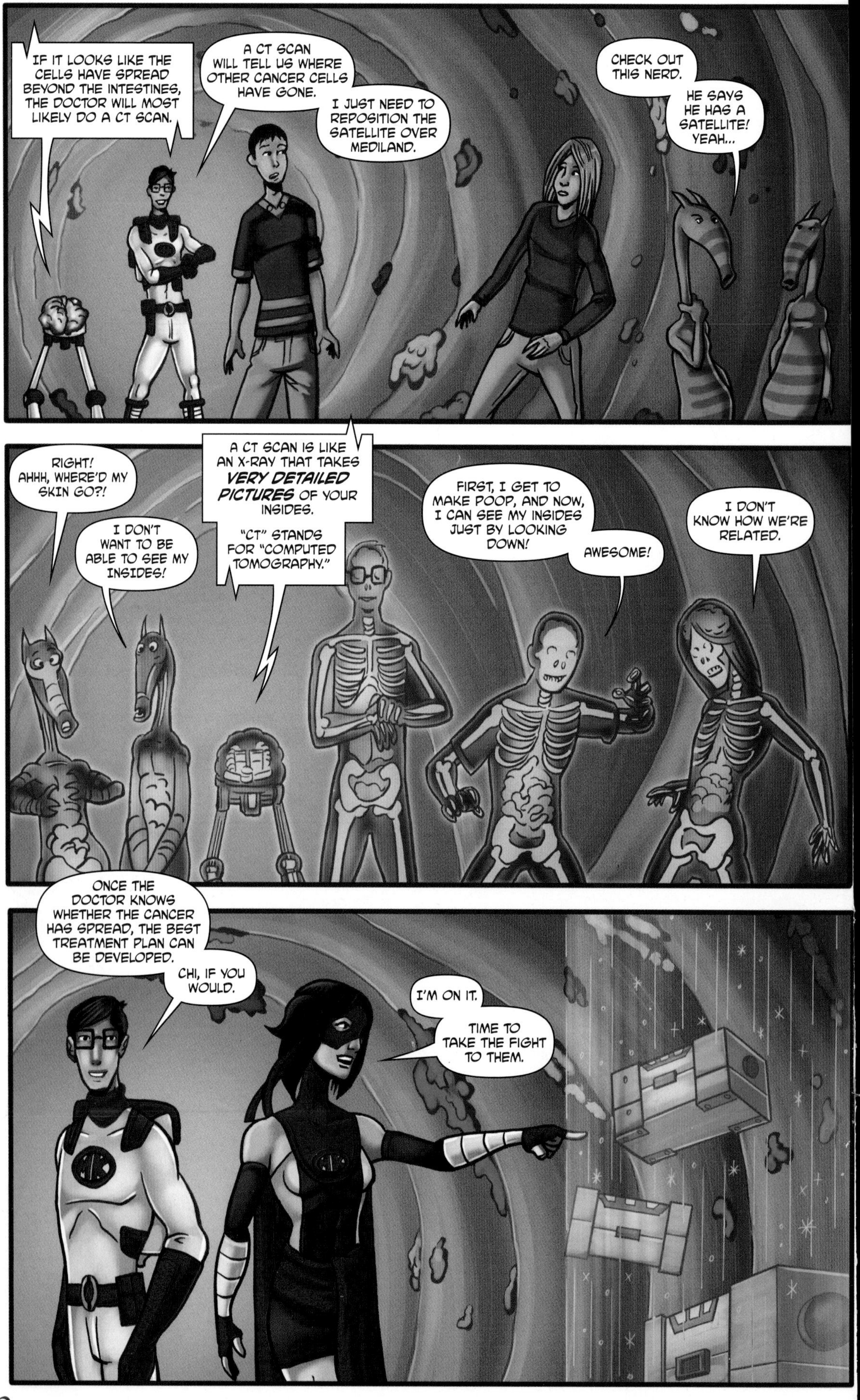
IF IT LOOKS LIKE THE CELLS HAVE SPREAD BEYOND THE INTESTINES, THE DOCTOR WILL MOST LIKELY DO A CT SCAN.
A CT SCAN WILL TELL US WHERE OTHER CANCER CELLS HAVE GONE.
I JUST NEED TO REPOSITION THE SATELLITE OVER MEDILAND.
CHECK OUT THIS NERD.
HE SAYS HE HAS A SATELLITE! YEAH...
RIGHT! AHHH, WHERE'D MY SKIN GO?!
I DON'T WANT TO BE ABLE TO SEE MY INSIDES!
A CT SCAN IS LIKE AN X-RAY THAT TAKES VERY DETAILED PICTURES OF YOUR INSIDES.
"CT" STANDS FOR "COMPUTED TOMOGRAPHY."
FIRST, I GET TO MAKE POOP, AND NOW, I CAN SEE MY INSIDES JUST BY LOOKING DOWN!
AWESOME!
I DON'T KNOW HOW WE'RE RELATED.
ONCE THE DOCTOR KNOWS WHETHER THE CANCER HAS SPREAD, THE BEST TREATMENT PLAN CAN BE DEVELOPED.
CHI, IF YOU WOULD.
I'M ON IT.
TIME TO TAKE THE FIGHT TO THEM.

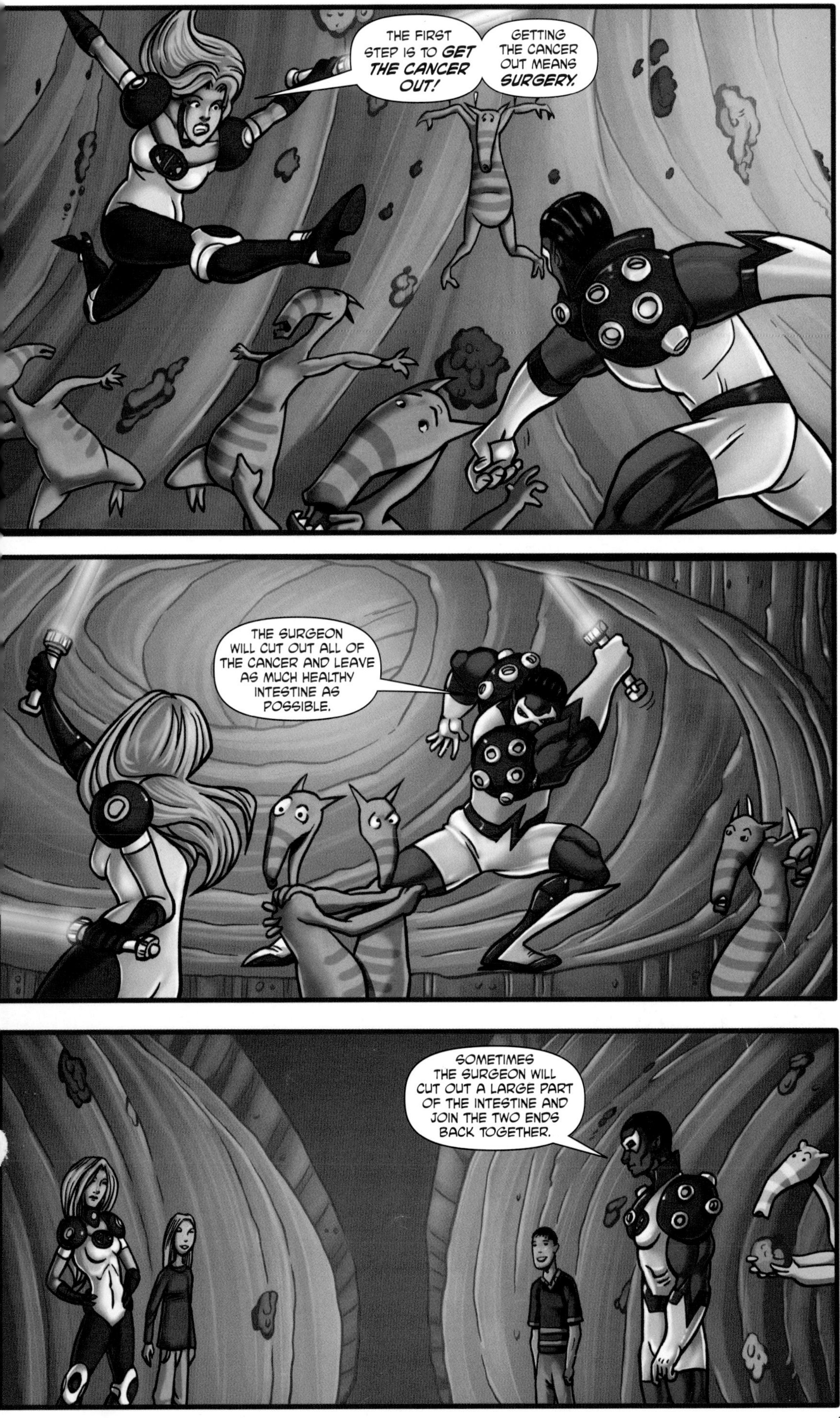
THE FIRST STEP IS TO **GET THE CANCER OUT!**
GETTING THE CANCER OUT MEANS **SURGERY.**
THE SURGEON WILL CUT OUT ALL OF THE CANCER AND LEAVE AS MUCH HEALTHY INTESTINE AS POSSIBLE.
SOMETIMES THE SURGEON WILL CUT OUT A LARGE PART OF THE INTESTINE AND JOIN THE TWO ENDS BACK TOGETHER.

IT'S NOT VERY COMMON, BUT IF THE CANCER IS NEAR THE END OF THE INTESTINE, OR IS TOO BIG, THE DOCTOR MAY NOT BE ABLE TO JOIN THE TWO ENDS TOGETHER!

IF THIS HAPPENS, THE DOCTOR WILL MAKE A *STOMA.*

A STOMA IS AN OPENING THE DOCTOR MAKES IN THE WALL OF THE BELLY. THE DOCTOR CAN THEN ATTACH THE INTESTINE TO THE SMALL OPENING.

AFTER THAT, THE DOCTOR...OR IN OUR CASE THE REMOTE CONTROLLED MEDI-JET...

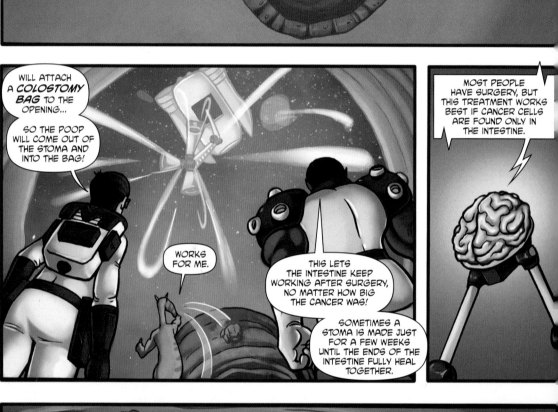

WILL ATTACH A *COLOSTOMY BAG* TO THE OPENING...

SO THE POOP WILL COME OUT OF THE STOMA AND INTO THE BAG!

WORKS FOR ME.

THIS LETS THE INTESTINE KEEP WORKING AFTER SURGERY, NO MATTER HOW BIG THE CANCER WAS!

SOMETIMES A STOMA IS MADE JUST FOR A FEW WEEKS UNTIL THE ENDS OF THE INTESTINE FULLY HEAL TOGETHER.

MOST PEOPLE HAVE SURGERY, BUT THIS TREATMENT WORKS BEST IF CANCER CELLS ARE FOUND ONLY IN THE INTESTINE.

AFTER SURGERY, A DOCTOR WILL LOOK AT THE CANCER MORE CLOSELY TO FIND OUT ITS STAGE.

THE STAGE SHOWS HOW BADLY THE CANCER CELLS ARE BEHAVING AND WHETHER THE CANCER HAS SPREAD.

I'LL SHOW YOU BAD BEHAVIOR, FOUR EYES!

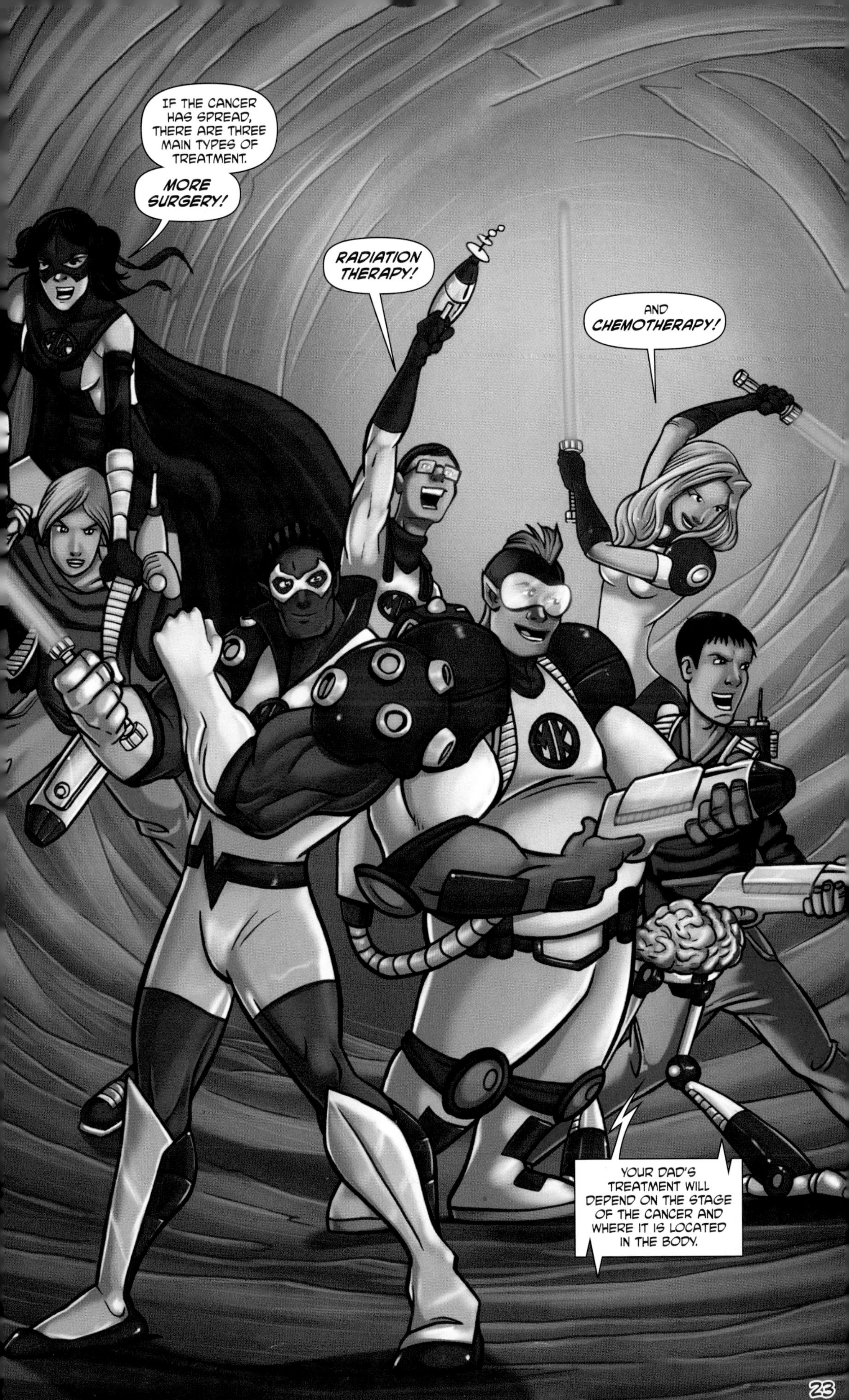
IF THE CANCER HAS SPREAD, THERE ARE THREE MAIN TYPES OF TREATMENT.
MORE SURGERY!
RADIATION THERAPY!
AND CHEMOTHERAPY!
YOUR DAD'S TREATMENT WILL DEPEND ON THE STAGE OF THE CANCER AND WHERE IT IS LOCATED IN THE BODY.

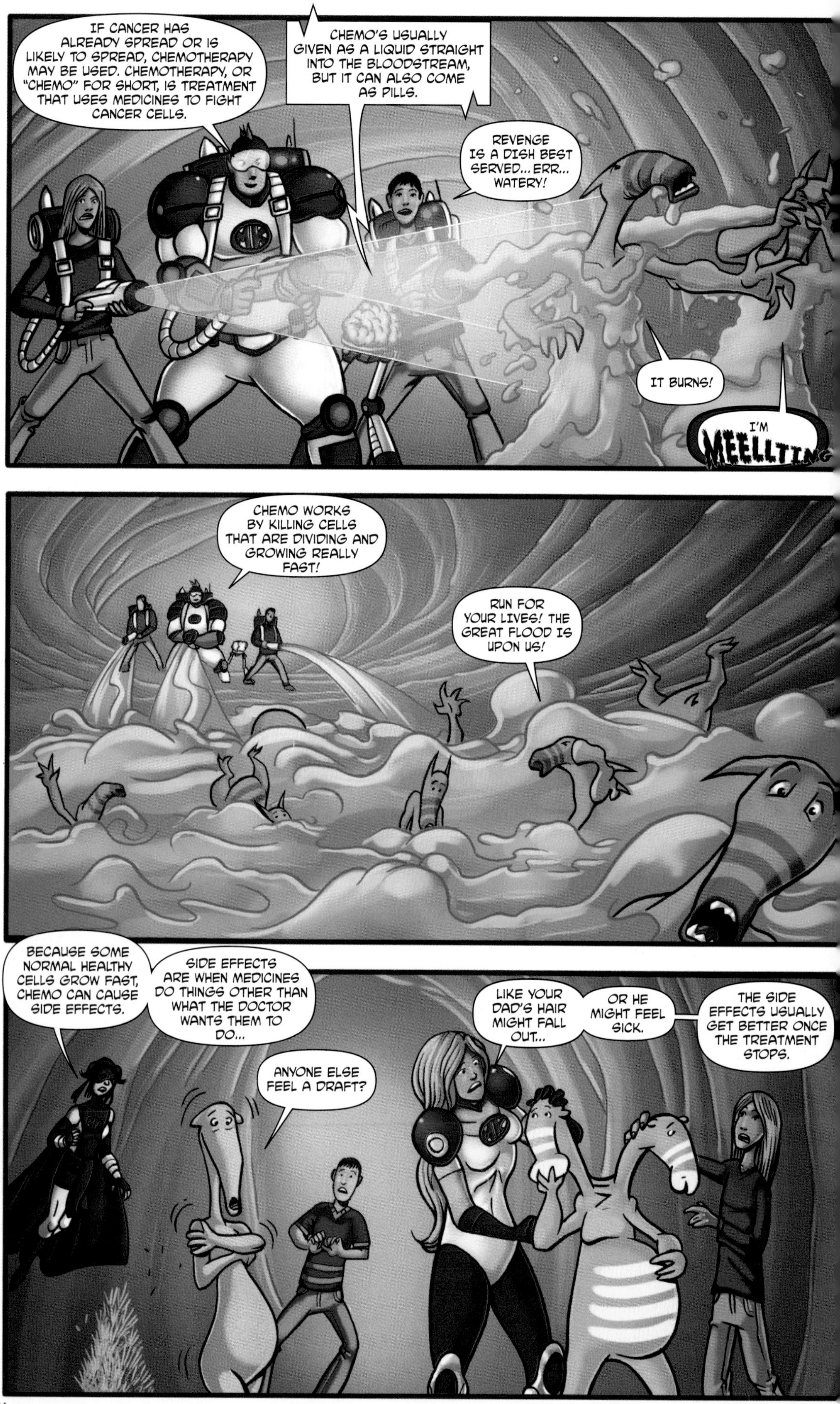

IF CANCER HAS ALREADY SPREAD OR IS LIKELY TO SPREAD, CHEMOTHERAPY MAY BE USED. CHEMOTHERAPY, OR "CHEMO" FOR SHORT, IS TREATMENT THAT USES MEDICINES TO FIGHT CANCER CELLS.
CHEMO'S USUALLY GIVEN AS A LIQUID STRAIGHT INTO THE BLOODSTREAM, BUT IT CAN ALSO COME AS PILLS.
REVENGE IS A DISH BEST SERVED... ERR... WATERY!
IT BURNS!
I'M MEELLTING
CHEMO WORKS BY KILLING CELLS THAT ARE DIVIDING AND GROWING REALLY FAST!
RUN FOR YOUR LIVES! THE GREAT FLOOD IS UPON US!
BECAUSE SOME NORMAL HEALTHY CELLS GROW FAST, CHEMO CAN CAUSE SIDE EFFECTS.
SIDE EFFECTS ARE WHEN MEDICINES DO THINGS OTHER THAN WHAT THE DOCTOR WANTS THEM TO DO...
ANYONE ELSE FEEL A DRAFT?
LIKE YOUR DAD'S HAIR MIGHT FALL OUT...
OR HE MIGHT FEEL SICK.
THE SIDE EFFECTS USUALLY GET BETTER ONCE THE TREATMENT STOPS.

ANOTHER TREATMENT OPTION IS *RADIATION THERAPY.*

RADIATION THERAPY USES POWERFUL *ENERGY RAYS* TO KILL CANCER CELLS.

IT'S POINTED *DIRECTLY* AT THE TUMOR AND KILLS THE CANCER CELLS THERE.

IT FEELS LIKE THE SUN IS MAD AT ME!

WHERE ARE YOU GUYS RUNNING TO? I THOUGHT WE WERE HAVING A BLAST!

HEH! MAN, I AM SO FUNNY!

UMMM, I CAN'T FEEL MY LEGS.

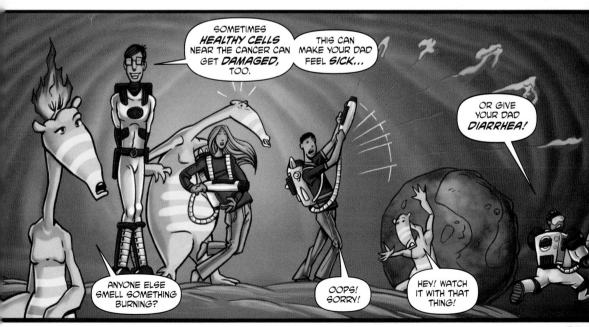

SOMETIMES *HEALTHY CELLS* NEAR THE CANCER CAN GET *DAMAGED,* TOO.

THIS CAN MAKE YOUR DAD FEEL *SICK...*

OR GIVE YOUR DAD *DIARRHEA!*

ANYONE ELSE SMELL SOMETHING BURNING?

OOPS! SORRY!

HEY! WATCH IT WITH THAT THING!

BUT, WHY IS THIS HAPPENING TO OUR DAD?

YEAH, IT'S NOT FAIR!

MOST OF THE TIME WE DON'T KNOW WHY PEOPLE GET COLORECTAL CANCER, BUT PEOPLE ARE MORE LIKELY TO GET COLORECTAL CANCER IF...

THEY ARE OVER 50...

I ONLY GET BETTER WITH AGE... AND BY BETTER I MEAN CRANKIER!

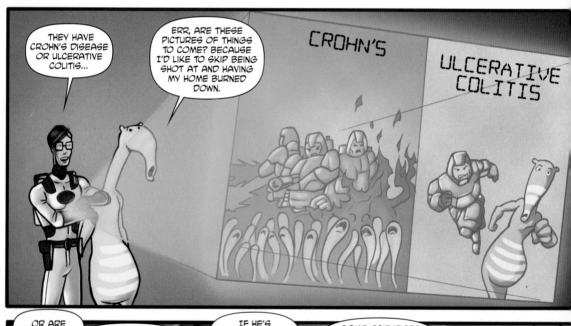

THEY HAVE CROHN'S DISEASE OR ULCERATIVE COLITIS...

ERR, ARE THESE PICTURES OF THINGS TO COME? BECAUSE I'D LIKE TO SKIP BEING SHOT AT AND HAVING MY HOME BURNED DOWN.

CROHN'S

ULCERATIVE COLITIS

OR ARE OVERWEIGHT!

HEY! HOW COME YOU GUYS HAD ME SAY THE OVERWEIGHT ONE?

IF HE'S LOOKING FOR THE REASON, I THINK IT'S IN THERE!

SOME SCIENTISTS ALSO THINK THAT TOO MUCH PROCESSED MEAT INCREASES A PERSON'S CHANCES OF GETTING COLORECTAL CANCER.

BUT SOME PEOPLE GET COLORECTAL CANCER WITHOUT HAVING ANY OF THESE RISK FACTORS.

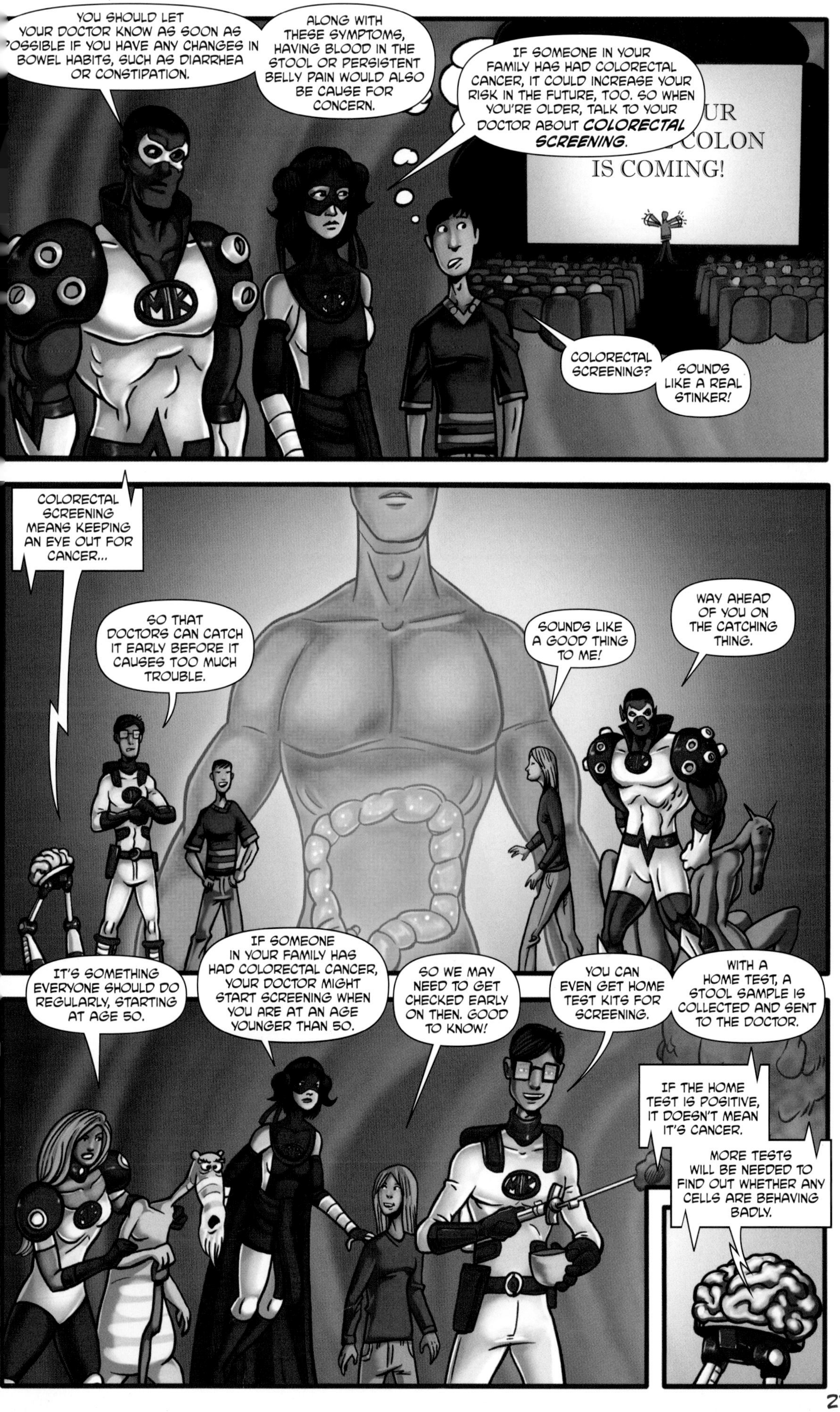

YOU SHOULD LET YOUR DOCTOR KNOW AS SOON AS POSSIBLE IF YOU HAVE ANY CHANGES IN BOWEL HABITS, SUCH AS DIARRHEA OR CONSTIPATION.
ALONG WITH THESE SYMPTOMS, HAVING BLOOD IN THE STOOL OR PERSISTENT BELLY PAIN WOULD ALSO BE CAUSE FOR CONCERN.
IF SOMEONE IN YOUR FAMILY HAS HAD COLORECTAL CANCER, IT COULD INCREASE YOUR RISK IN THE FUTURE, TOO. SO WHEN YOU'RE OLDER, TALK TO YOUR DOCTOR ABOUT ***COLORECTAL SCREENING***.
IS COMING!
COLORECTAL SCREENING?
SOUNDS LIKE A REAL STINKER!
COLORECTAL SCREENING MEANS KEEPING AN EYE OUT FOR CANCER...
SO THAT DOCTORS CAN CATCH IT EARLY BEFORE IT CAUSES TOO MUCH TROUBLE.
SOUNDS LIKE A GOOD THING TO ME!
WAY AHEAD OF YOU ON THE CATCHING THING.
IT'S SOMETHING EVERYONE SHOULD DO REGULARLY, STARTING AT AGE 50.
IF SOMEONE IN YOUR FAMILY HAS HAD COLORECTAL CANCER, YOUR DOCTOR MIGHT START SCREENING WHEN YOU ARE AT AN AGE YOUNGER THAN 50.
SO WE MAY NEED TO GET CHECKED EARLY ON THEN. GOOD TO KNOW!
YOU CAN EVEN GET HOME TEST KITS FOR SCREENING.
WITH A HOME TEST, A STOOL SAMPLE IS COLLECTED AND SENT TO THE DOCTOR.
IF THE HOME TEST IS POSITIVE, IT DOESN'T MEAN IT'S CANCER.
MORE TESTS WILL BE NEEDED TO FIND OUT WHETHER ANY CELLS ARE BEHAVING BADLY.

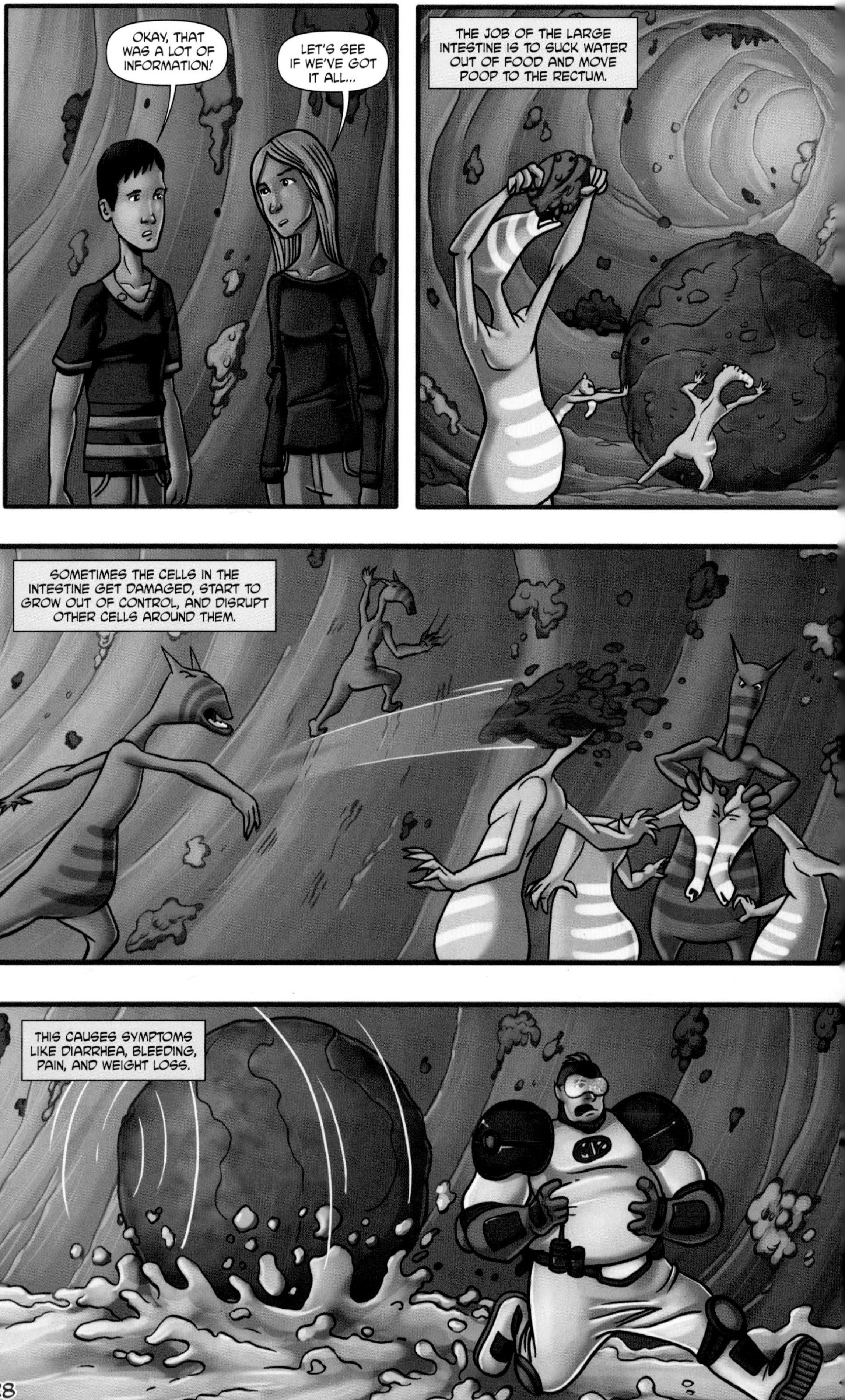

OKAY, THAT WAS A LOT OF INFORMATION!
LET'S SEE IF WE'VE GOT IT ALL...
THE JOB OF THE LARGE INTESTINE IS TO SUCK WATER OUT OF FOOD AND MOVE POOP TO THE RECTUM.
SOMETIMES THE CELLS IN THE INTESTINE GET DAMAGED, START TO GROW OUT OF CONTROL, AND DISRUPT OTHER CELLS AROUND THEM.
THIS CAUSES SYMPTOMS LIKE DIARRHEA, BLEEDING, PAIN, AND WEIGHT LOSS.

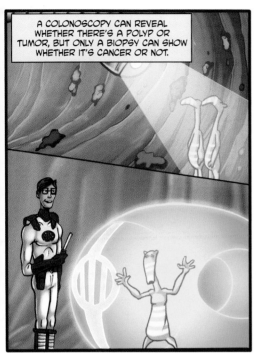

A COLONOSCOPY CAN REVEAL WHETHER THERE'S A POLYP OR TUMOR, BUT ONLY A BIOPSY CAN SHOW WHETHER IT'S CANCER OR NOT.

TREATMENT OPTIONS INCLUDE SURGERY, CHEMOTHERAPY, AND/OR RADIATION THERAPY, DEPENDING ON THE STAGE OF THE CANCER.

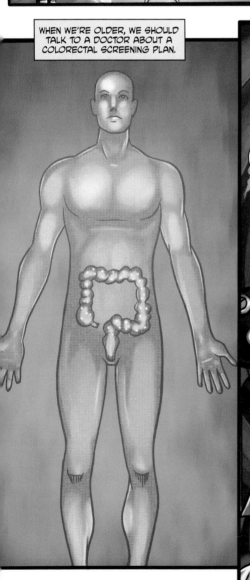

WHEN WE'RE OLDER, WE SHOULD TALK TO A DOCTOR ABOUT A COLORECTAL SCREENING PLAN.

YOU NAILED IT!

I KNEW YOU WOULD!

THANKS, MEDIKIDZ!

IT'S GREAT TO FINALLY UNDERSTAND WHAT'S GOING ON WITH OUR DAD.

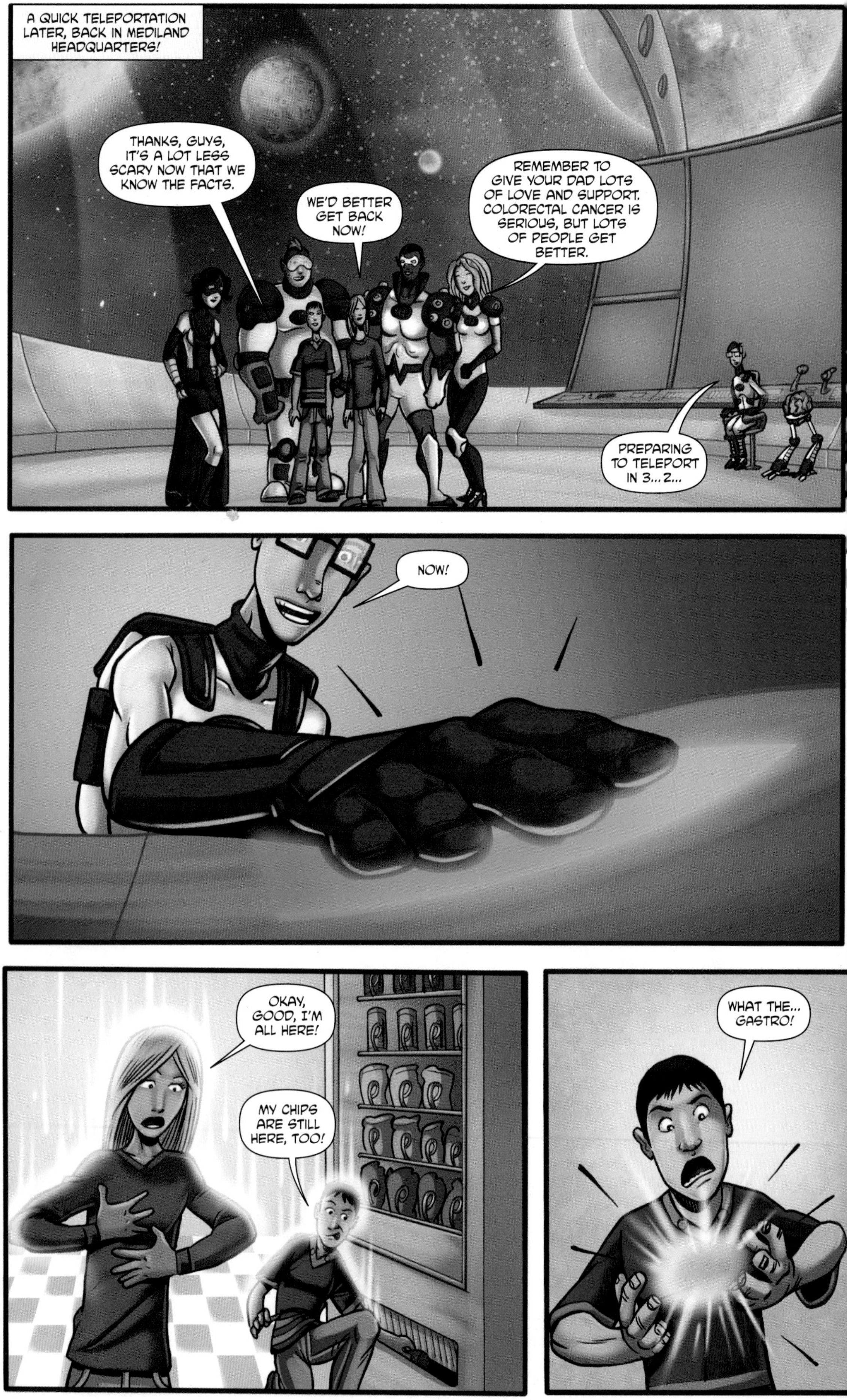
A QUICK TELEPORTATION LATER, BACK IN MEDILAND HEADQUARTERS!
THANKS, GUYS, IT'S A LOT LESS SCARY NOW THAT WE KNOW THE FACTS.
WE'D BETTER GET BACK NOW!
REMEMBER TO GIVE YOUR DAD LOTS OF LOVE AND SUPPORT. COLORECTAL CANCER IS SERIOUS, BUT LOTS OF PEOPLE GET BETTER.
PREPARING TO TELEPORT IN 3...2...
NOW!
OKAY, GOOD, I'M ALL HERE!
MY CHIPS ARE STILL HERE, TOO!
WHAT THE... GASTRO!

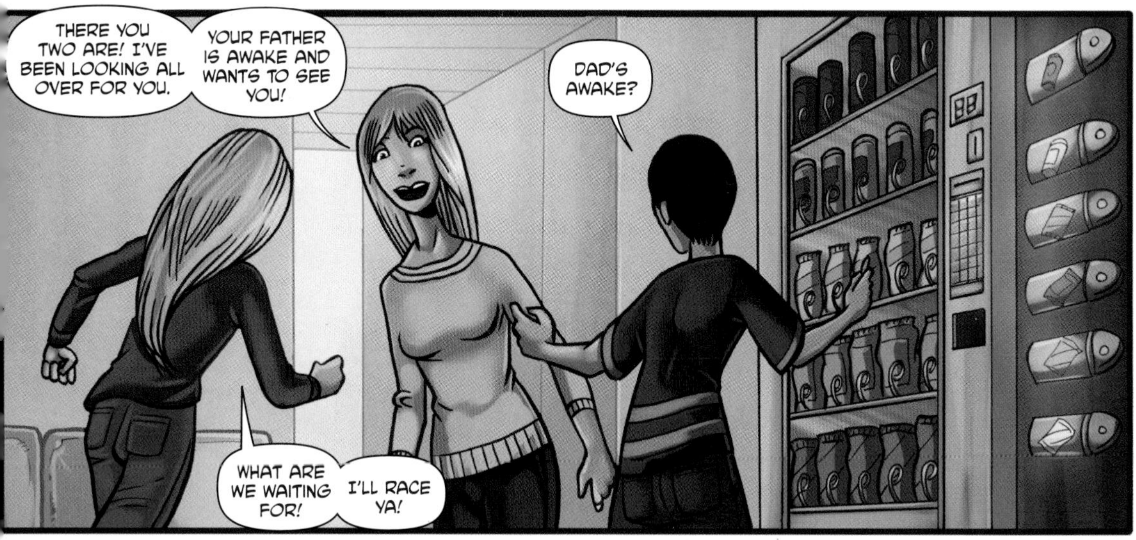
THERE YOU TWO ARE! I'VE BEEN LOOKING ALL OVER FOR YOU.
YOUR FATHER IS AWAKE AND WANTS TO SEE YOU!
DAD'S AWAKE?
WHAT ARE WE WAITING FOR!
I'LL RACE YA!

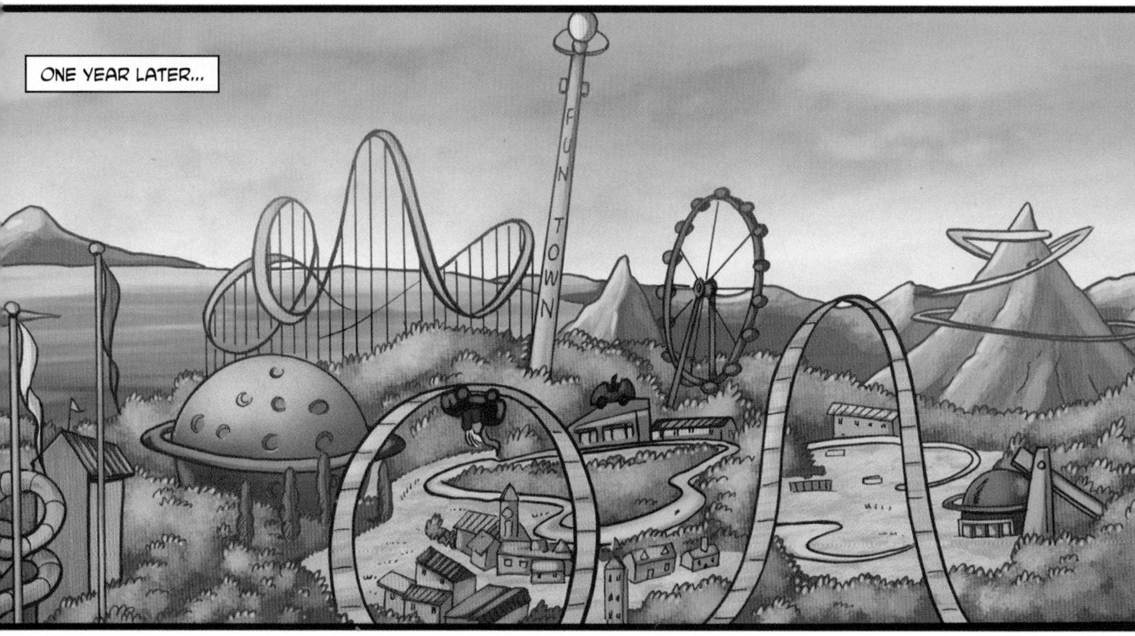
ONE YEAR LATER...
FUN TOWN

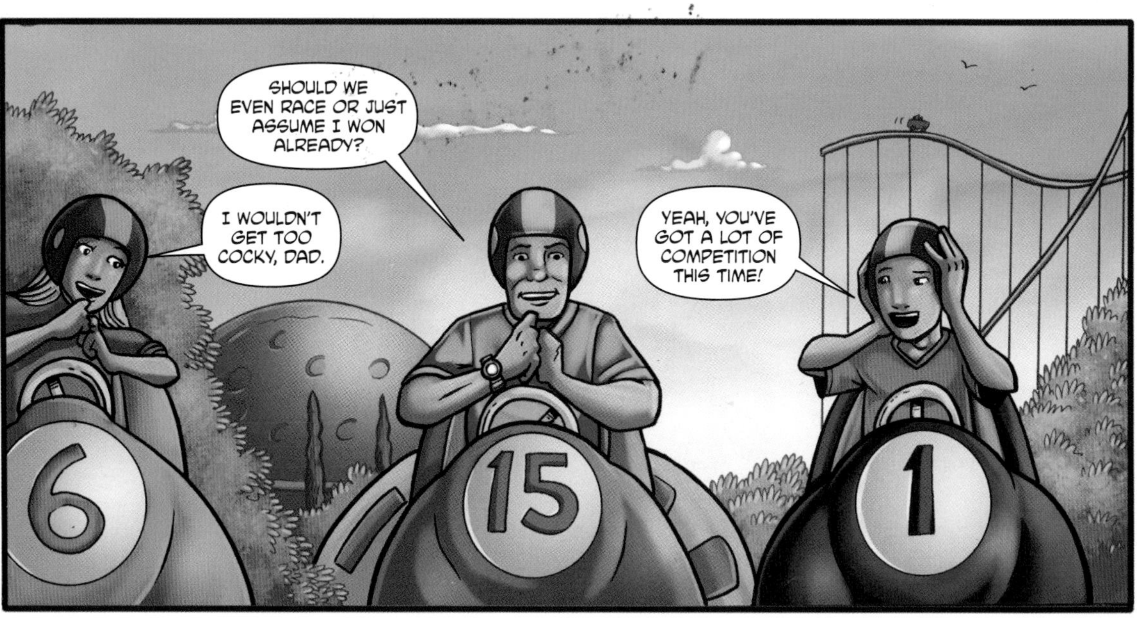
SHOULD WE EVEN RACE OR JUST ASSUME I WON ALREADY?
I WOULDN'T GET TOO COCKY, DAD.
YEAH, YOU'VE GOT A LOT OF COMPETITION THIS TIME!
6
15
1

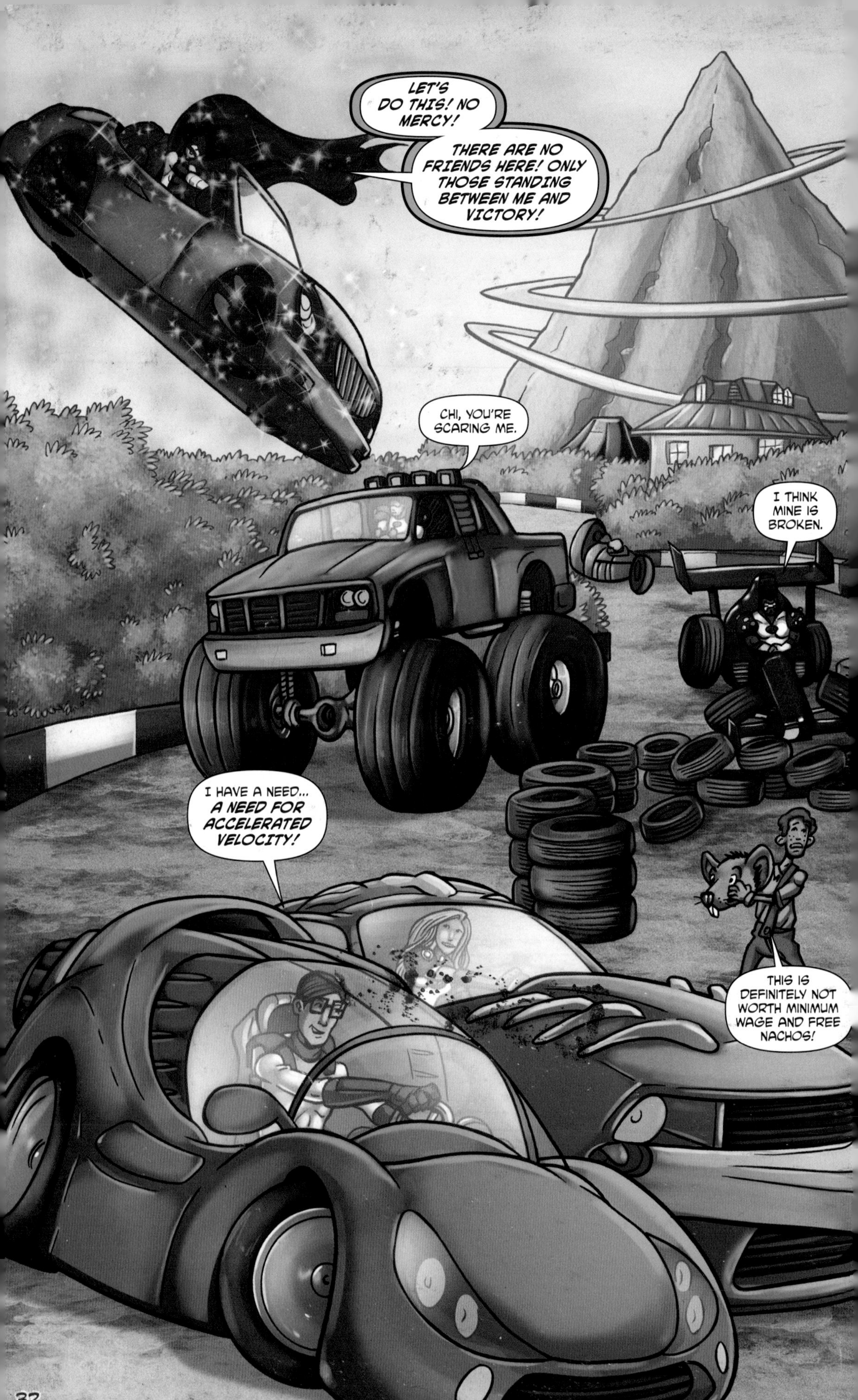
LET'S DO THIS! NO MERCY!
THERE ARE NO FRIENDS HERE! ONLY THOSE STANDING BETWEEN ME AND VICTORY!
CHI, YOU'RE SCARING ME.
I THINK MINE IS BROKEN.
I HAVE A NEED... A NEED FOR ACCELERATED VELOCITY!
THIS IS DEFINITELY NOT WORTH MINIMUM WAGE AND FREE NACHOS!